"It's easy for ministry leaders to cast a vision but tough to keep it sharply focused over time. In *Be Mean About the Vision: Preserving and Protecting What Matters*, Shawn Lovejoy reveals what's required to avoid the distractions, disruptions, and divisions we face when pursuing our priorities. Drawing on his vast experience working with pastors and church leaders, he shares insightful biblical wisdom for keeping teams unified and on track. This book is a must-read for anyone wanting to be a Christlike leader."

CHRIS HODGES, SENIOR PASTOR,
CHURCH OF THE HIGHLANDS;
AUTHOR OF *FRESH AIR* AND *FOUR CUPS*

"Shawn has given us a fresh book on vision! Shawn's principles are based on the realities of leadership in the local church he founded, built, and served so well for sixteen years. This book is from a leader who understands leadership. The stories are candid and the insights are practical. *Be Mean About the Vision: Preserving and Protecting What Matters* will help you clarify and lead your own vision at a new level!"

DAN REILAND, EXECUTIVE PASTOR,
12STONE CHURCH, LAWRENCEVILLE, GA

"The first time I heard Shawn give his talk, 'Be Mean About the Vision,' I knew he had to turn it into a book. Now a few years later he has done all church leaders a service by helping leaders to shape, clarify, defend, and steward God's call for a church as expressed by a vision. And Shawn is right—you have to learn to 'be mean' in order for it to animate others toward positive results. While vision is often high minded and theoretical, this is a very practical and helpful work."

DAVE TRAVIS, CEO, LEADERSHIP NETWORK

"If a leader isn't 'mean' about the vision it won't be long until inertia, mission creep, and human nature drown it out. In *Be Mean About the Vision*, Shawn shows us in down-to-earth, practical terms what it takes to find, clarify, and ensure that the main thing remains the main thing over the long haul."

LARRY OSBORNE, AUTHOR;
PASTOR OF NORTH COAST CHURCH, VISTA, CA

"Shawn's focused willingness has written a pretty remarkable story today that continues even though he's no longer the lead pastor of my church. It's embedded deep in the bones of Mountain Lake thanks to the incredible sacrifice of Shawn. Know, as you're reading this book, that this isn't pie in the sky. It's a reality. It's possible for you to implement a culture and vision at your church that people will write about too, if you will be mean about the vision."

BLAKE STANLEY, PASTOR OF MINISTRIES,
MOUNTAIN LAKE CHURCH, CUMMING, GA

"In a noisy world that's crowded with distractions, focus might be the best asset of a leader. Shawn's focus is the reason his church is doing well. Smart leaders will focus on this book, and learn to be mean about the vision God has given them."

WILLIAM VANDERBLOEMEN, FOUNDER AND
PRESIDENT, VANDERBLOEMEN SEARCH GROUP

"It's more than a catchy book title. *Be Mean About the Vision: Preserving and Protecting What Matters* is the essence of what it takes to lead an organization—sacred or secular. Locations, staffing, programming, budgeting, delivery systems are all negotiables, but not vision. Change, downsize, or dilute the vision and you will create another organization altogether. Shawn Lovejoy will share with great transparency the upside as well as the underbelly of what it really means to preserve and protect what matters."

SAM CHAND, LEADERSHIP CONSULTANT,
AUTHOR OF *LEADERSHIP PAIN*

"One of the defining characteristics of Shawn's leadership through the years has been his passion for clarity about keeping people focused on the thing that matters most in every organization: the vision. This book will give you the courage you need to point your organization at a vision worthy of your best."

MATT KELLER, LEADERSHIP COACH, PASTOR,
AUTHOR OF *THE KEY TO EVERYTHING*

"Shawn's honest writing of his own leadership story challenges leaders to wrestle with the vision God has uniquely given to them—and see it through with courage."

TONY MORGAN, FOUNDER AND CHIEF
STRATEGIC OFFICER, THE UNSTUCK GROUP

NEXT
LEADERSHIP NETWORK

BE MEAN ABOUT THE VISION

PRESERVING AND PROTECTING WHAT MATTERS

SHAWN LOVEJOY

THOMAS NELSON
Since 1798

Published in Nashville, Tennessee, by Thomas Nelson. Thomas Nelson is a registered trademark of HarperCollins Christian Publishing.

Thomas Nelson titles may be purchased in bulk for educational, business, fund-raising, or sales promotional use. For information, please e-mail SpecialMarkets@ThomasNelson.com.

Library of Congress Control Number: 2014959032

Softcover: 978-0718-0328-8-3

e-Book: 978-0718-0328-9-0

Printed in the United States of America
16 17 18 19 20 RRD 6 5 4 3 2 1

CONTENTS

About Leadership ✖ Network

Leadership Network fosters innovation movements that activate the church to greater impact. We help shape the conversations and practices of pacesetter churches in North America and around the world. The Leadership Network mind-set identifies church leaders with forward-thinking ideas—and helps them to catalyze those ideas resulting in movements that shape the church.

Together with HarperCollins Christian Publishing, the biggest name in Christian books, the NEXT imprint of Leadership Network moves ideas to implementation for leaders to take their ideas to form, substance, and reality. Placed in the hands of other church leaders, that reality begins spreading from one leader to the next . . . and to the next . . . and to the next, where that idea begins to flourish into a full-grown movement that creates a real, tangible impact in the world around it.

**NEXT: A Leadership Network Resource
committed to helping you grow your next idea.**

leadnet.org/NEXT

FOREWORD

Vision is an odd thing.

Some Christian leaders find vision to be elusive. Others have great ideas about vision but are unable to apply them. And then there are leaders who think vision isn't important as long as they are faithful and work hard at ministry.

Vision isn't something I was taught in seminary, but after thirty years of vocational ministry, I have found it to be essential in the church. Vision matters deeply. The right vision can transform the life of a church. However, vision may be one of the most neglected areas in the local church.

Let me be clear: I don't think vision is the answer to everything.

If you don't have a church that focuses on the gospel, values Scripture, and follows Jesus and relies on the power of the Holy Spirit, you can have a compelling vision that takes you to the wrong location. But on more than one occasion, I have seen the difference between two churches filled with people who love

Jesus—one that has caught and held the vision and the other that has not.

Casting vision is one thing, but vision without the ability to back it up ultimately becomes a pipe dream. When vision is correctly applied to a church body and is undergirded by biblical values, integrity, and authenticity, it becomes a powerful motivator to mobilize people and ultimately to change the world.

Shawn Lovejoy has identified one of the biggest challenges any leader faces: how to gather people around a vision and stay true to that vision. I met Shawn over a decade ago. We visited with one another, shared common friends, and grew a friendship as we served in the same town. Shawn loves Jesus, his family, and the church. He has a passion for leading people closer to God and then sending them out to live on mission every day. He genuinely cares for people. I'd go as far as to say that there's not a mean bone in his body. (Although Shawn might disagree with me and say there's at least one mean bone.) As he often says: "You should be mean about one thing; be mean about the vision."

I've quoted Shawn about this on more than one occasion. But as I began to observe Shawn, I noticed his meanness wasn't meanness in the sense of being unkind. It was simply firmness, and his firmness was essential to his success of growing a great church and mobilizing a people for a great purpose.

You see, that's what vision does. Vision gathers people together for a common purpose so they might be focused on something greater than themselves. Vision is essential in so many areas of life. In business, CEOs cast vision around a product or resource to bring satisfaction to the customer and profit to the business. In government, politicians cast a vision for a better tomorrow around themes of change and hope. In the military, generals rally their troops with a vision of victory. In all these places, resources, tools, and training exist to help leaders more effectively cast that vision. Yet those same resources are often lacking in the church.

Be Mean About the Vision helps remedy that situation. In this book, you'll be encouraged and equipped to not only develop and articulate a vision for your church but also to hold fast to that vision.

Every church member and staff member who comes through your doors has a vision for your church. Those visions aren't all bad. And as your church grows and leadership multiplies, the vision will become more collaborative and shared across a large organization. But the reality is, leaders cast vision.

When we look at Exodus 18, probably the most famous passage on leadership in the Bible, certain things were delegated to the leaders of tens, fifties, hundreds, and thousands, but the teaching and the direction stayed in the hands of Moses.

Shawn points us to a model of leadership that calls us to cast a compelling vision, evaluate and modify as necessary, to guard that vision against those who might hijack it, and lead people forward in that vision. Shawn challenges us to recognize that, as leaders, God has gifted us not only with a role but with a responsibility—to be mean about the vision.

Ed Stetzer, PhD
LifeWay Research
edstetzer.com

ACKNOWLEDGMENTS

I want to first thank my wife and my ministry partner, Tricia, for twenty plus years of following God's vision for our lives. I'm also grateful for Hannah, Madison, and Paul, who have always been by our side as we have sought to follow God's vision for our lives and ministry. I'm eternally grateful to both the ministry team and the congregation at Mountain Lake Church. Thanks for staying true to the vision! For sixteen years, our church was a textbook example of being mean about the vision. Thank you! Finally, I am thankful for the team at Thomas Nelson and Leadership Network for helping get sixteen years of jumbled thoughts and teachings into an organized, comprehensive guide on vision. Thanks for being my partners!

ONE

BEING MEAN

I don't consider myself to be a mean person. And I don't think most people around me would say I'm mean. I like to think I'm good with people. I'm mostly an extrovert. I'm a neck hugger. I regularly tell people I love them. I try to draw people out and show them I care. Of course I'm not perfect, and I have been known to act or speak in ways God might not always be proud of, but I like to think meanness is not a major characteristic of my personality.

Are you a mean leader? You may have picked up this book thinking I was going to give you permission to be a mean person. Frankly, though, there are too many mean leaders out there today. And, believe it or not, this is true especially in ministry! Regardless of where we all are on the *mean* spectrum, being mean about the vision is not about being mean to people. In fact, it's exactly the opposite.

> Being mean about the vision is not about being mean to people. In fact, it's exactly the opposite.

1

In the sense I'm talking about, being "mean" is actually the best thing we could do for the people we lead. Being mean about the vision could even be described as "spiritual" and "godly." It ensures that everyone understands, embraces, is inspired by, and is unified around the vision for the organizations we lead.

If you look up the word *mean* in the dictionary, you'll see several definitions. One of them says that to be mean is "to be offensive, selfish, or unaccommodating."[1] That's the definition most of us think of first; but if you think more about it, that is not even the most common use of the word *mean* itself. The other definition of the word *mean* is "to have an intended purpose."[2] In this instance, the word *mean* has to do with intent. We'll say, "I didn't *mean* that," or "I *meant* that as a compliment," or "What I *meant* to say was . . ." This is how we use the word most often. And for the purposes of this book, this is what "being mean" is all about. Being "mean" about the vision is being intentional about the vision. It's purposefully protecting the vision over time. Being mean about the vision is living it out daily in our lives, keeping our hearts focused and aligned with it. It's communicating that vision with clarity and energy. Being mean is moving in a consistent direction, and recognizing when the vision begins to drift. When you're mean about the vision, you will also protect it at all costs. You won't allow what I call "vision hijackers"—people who want to derail the vision—to throw things off course. When you're mean about the vision, you'll *intentionally* keep the vision as the epicenter of all you are and all you do.

Here's the deal: If we're not intentional about the vision, we will lose it. We will drift off course. We will end up going somewhere we don't want to go and becoming something we don't want to become. We will end up wasting our time. Our organizations will cease to fulfill the purposes for which they were created. If that happens, our organizations will slowly lose their usefulness, until they eventually die. Anyone want to sign up for that?

On the other hand, maintaining the vision over time leads to success. If we see the vision through, we have been successful. We've accomplished our purpose.

Everyone starts out with a vision, but few finish with one. This book is about finishing with vision. There is no greater fulfillment in life than to know the vision God gave you is being accomplished. If you're at the start of something new, or at a turning point in your life or the life of your organization, this book will help you shepherd everyone across the finish line of success together. If you've been at it a while and your vision has lost its vitality, this book is for you. If you question whether your organization or your leaders are with you and behind you, this book is for you. If you're fighting on the front lines to maintain the vision, this book is for you. And even if the vision has died inside of you, this book is most certainly for you!

> Everyone starts out with a vision,
> but few finish with one.

Every organization I've ever come across started with a reasonably good vision. They want to do something that's never been done. To invent something that has not been invented. To go where no one has been. To provide something that no one else is providing.

In churches, it's to reach who no one else is reaching—to make a difference the way no one else has. All of these are good and godly pursuits. But the reality is, most organizations never do what they really set out to do. They don't change the world. They don't even change their own community.

Too many organizations have lost their way over time. They got sidetracked. They forgot why they existed. When we forget *why* we do *what* we do, we'll eventually lose our passion. It happens slowly and quietly. Rarely can anyone point to a specific day when vision left the building. Nonetheless, in these organizations, the vision was lost. Everyone forgot why they were there in the first place.

Maybe you have lost the passion that used to keep you going. Maybe you've lost that spark—that momentum. You feel stuck. The organization seems to be trudging uphill, or worse yet, everything is going downhill and no one understands why. The leaders in your group are frustrated, disillusioned, and discouraged. The members, employees, or stockholders are nervous and restless. Everyone seems lost. You might say to yourself, "How did we end up here? How did we get so far off course?"

Is this something you've experienced? Or would you like to keep from experiencing it? This book is about making sure this scenario never happens, or that it never happens again. If you're currently in the midst of losing your vision, you'll learn here how to get it back. You'll learn how to dust it off, tune it up, and get it running again, firing on all cylinders. And most important, you'll learn how to protect it this time.

WHAT WE NEED TO LEARN ABOUT VISION

In the pages that follow, we will talk about the most important, compelling subject on the planet: vision. We're going to talk about what it is, how to find it, how to live it, how to communicate it, how to keep it, how to discover it when we've lost it, how to protect it when it's attacked, and how to see it through to the end. We're going to discover how to *be mean* about the vision. This is the work of my life. I pray you will see this whole journey through to the end with me.

I was founding and lead pastor of Mountain Lake Church in Cumming, Georgia, for sixteen years. I'll tell about my experiences there throughout this book, including how I passed the baton to my successor and stepped into a new vision for my life. (Yes, it happened to me, and can happen to you! More on that later.) But after all that time leading at Mountain Lake, I can say that I am most proud of three things: my wife still likes me (and loves me, as well); my kids love the church (not just the church I pastored, but *the* church); and during my entire tenure, our church stayed true to its original vision. For all those years, we did not waver. We stayed laser-beam focused. We never allowed our church to turn into a Christian country club for the "frozen chosen." And the church is still going strong even after my departure—because the church was formed around a mission, not a man! Looking back over my time there, I'm amazed that the church was just as unified on the day I left as it was when it first started in our living room. Keeping the vision focused and aligned was not always easy. In fact, it never was! Maintaining the church's focus on the vision was always the most difficult task of leadership for me, and it will be for you too.

Why should you listen to what I have to say about vision? Great question. I am not the perfect leader. I have never walked on water. I have made thousands of leadership mistakes. I still do! Your organization may be larger or smaller than the ones I have led. That doesn't matter. What matters—regardless of an organization's size—is whether it stays focused or loses its way. I believe God gifted me as leader in this area, and I give Him all the glory for that gift. I have done it, and I have both the scars and the fruit to show it. Whether vision comes easily or difficult for you, I believe I can help you.

As cofounder and former directional leader for churchplanters.com and the Velocity Pastor's Network, I've had the privilege of speaking to and coaching hundreds of leaders in their endeavors to launch, protect, or reclaim their vision. Through our annual Velocity conference for pastors, and at conferences around the country, I've spoken to thousands of pastors about what I am going to share with you in the pages that follow. Much of the content you are about to read has been tried and tested for over a decade now in churches and other organizations across America and across the world. I have also consulted with many CEOs and business owners about the same issue: How do we keep everyone pulling in the same direction?

A few years back, my friend Ed Stetzer, president of LifeWay's research division, spoke at the Velocity conference, which was hosted at Mountain Lake. More than a hundred volunteers from the church helped pull off this two-day event that hosts close to a thousand pastors annually. Ed had heard me speak about being mean about the vision in one of the early sessions. I'll admit, I had boasted about my church family at Mountain Lake. I even said, "You probably can't find one person in our church who doesn't know and understand our mission." Ed took this as a personal challenge while on our church campus. He started his own private research project. Over the next couple of days at the conference, he made it his personal business to approach almost every volunteer with a simple question: "What is this church's mission? Tell me why this church exists." At the end of the day, Ed came clean and told me about his little research project. He concluded by saying, "I've never been around a church where every single person seems to not only *know* the mission, but was so passionate about *telling* me they knew!"

It's one thing to have a mission. It's quite another thing to get everyone to know it, embrace it, live it, and be passionate about it. I can honestly say that up until the day that I left, the people at Mountain Lake not only knew the mission; they embraced it and lived it unlike any place I have ever seen. The mission statement printed on the walls happened down the halls . . . and outside our walls—reaching thousands of people on multiple campuses in our community and impacting hundreds of churches around our nation and our world! I can trace all of our success, however, back to the vision.

Has this vision ever been threatened? You bet. Has the vision ever been questioned? Of course. Were we ever tempted to forget the vision? What do you think? I have actually had people say to me: "Well, Shawn, it's easy for you to talk about keeping an organization unified around the vision. You started your church." But trust me—it's not that easy. Sixteen years ago, our church was the new show in town. Before we even had our grand-opening day, dozens of people showed up with lots of good ideas about what we should be and do. People had ideas about programs, ministries, and events. A lot of them were good ideas. There were also lots of bad ones. In the early days, we had to be extremely careful what we listened to—and whom we listened to. We said yes many times, but also had to say, "Thanks, but no thanks," hundreds of times just during the first year. When you say yes to an event or program, do you know how long it takes to turn it into a tradition? It's instantaneous! If you say yes one time, inevitably people want to perpetuate the program until Jesus comes back (and maybe after)!

I'll never forget the year we did a message series called Building the Body. It's not what you think. The series was actually all about building and protecting unity in the church, the body of Christ. We wanted to add some fun to the series, so we thought we would also build up our physical bodies while we talked about building the spiritual body. We decided to hold a 5K race at the end of the message series. It was a *huge* success. Hundreds in our community participated. It was a lot of fun, and it served its purpose well.

After the race was over our volunteer coordinator for the event, who happened to be an avid runner, approached me to say: "This was awesome! We need to get the date on the calendar for next year's race now! We *are* doing this again next year, right?"

"No," I answered. "The race served a very specific purpose this year. Our church is not in the race business. We are in the church body business."

She did not like my answer and ended up leaving the church because we would not perpetuate a 5K race!

Over the years, we had to kill many sacred cows. We had to bury both good programs and ineffective programs and bring an end to ineffective ministries. We have said no to many things before they even got a chance to get started, simply because they were not in line with the vision. In fact, the best time to stop an off-vision program is before it gets started. It's always easier to say no now and yes later than it is to say yes now and no later. The latter is much more painful.

> The best time to stop an off-vision program is before it gets started.

Our church fought like any other organization to stay focused on the vision, even while experiencing periods of rapid growth. The faster an organization grows, the easier it is to get off track and lose its way. Every time new people join an organization, it takes them a while to gain perspective. And while things like "vision statements" are important, they never solve this problem completely.

VISION STATEMENTS ARE A DIME A DOZEN

To be honest, I'm not a big fan of vision statements. Vision statements are a dime a dozen as far as I'm concerned. Everyone these days has a vision statement. A few years ago, everyone had a "2020 Vision." Soon it will be a "2050 Vision," and so on. At the end of the day, however, a vision statement is just a *statement*. It has no life on its own. It cannot, nor will it ever, energize, unify, or align an organization. This task falls to the leader. A vision statement is only as strong as the leader is. Vision is only as clear as the leader is. Vision is only as compelling as a leader makes it. A vision is stewarded and sustained by a leader.

Over the years, much has been made about the differences between a *mission* and a *vision*. I actually use the terms interchangeably in this book. When you get right down to it, working leaders don't have time or energy to debate the difference between a mission and a vision. The best leaders devote their energy to inspiring people to unify around something—anything—that will move the organization in the direction they feel led to take it. If you're reading this, I'd venture to say that these three questions are all you care about: *Where are we going now? Where do we want to go? How do we take everyone there?* These are the real, relevant, and crucial questions we must answer.

A vision or mission serves the same purpose: It defines why we exist. No matter what we call it, being mean about the vision requires that we answer one question at the outset: "Why are we here?" That's really all we need to know in the beginning. Let's not cloud the issue with any other discussions until we can answer that one. If we're fortunate, we'll be able to get our organizations rallied and unified around that *one thing*. The vision is our goal. The vision is our bull's-eye. Let's keep it simple. Being mean about the vision is about keeping our organization so focused on the goal that people are willing to sacrifice for it. If we get that right, everything else will fall in place.

Having a vision statement is just a small slice of the pie. It's one thing to *say* we have a vision. It's another thing to live it out. That's where being mean about the vision comes in.

> It's one thing to *say* we have a vision.
> It's another thing to live it out.

My prayer through our time together is that God would give you a vision not only for your life but also for the organization you lead. My prayer is that God would also give you the clarity and the strength to be as mean as you need to be—until God does everything He wants to do in and through you and your organization.

In My Journal

I've always found that writing in a journal helps me better absorb the events of a busy day, along with the new ideas I encounter. Throughout this book, I'll offer some questions for reflection that will help you apply the key principles in each chapter. I hope you'll take some time to consider how these ideas might play out in your organization.

▶ Does everyone in my organization know our vision?

▶ Is everyone passionate about the vision? Why or why not?

▶ Where are we going?

▶ Where do we want to go?

▶ How can we take everyone with us?

TWO

IT ALL STARTS
WITH VISION

My wife, Tricia, and I, along with our then six-month-old daughter, Hannah, moved to metro Atlanta in 1999 to start a new church. As it is with any new vision, I was scared to death, but I had so much fire in my bones I couldn't be quiet or sit still. The longer we don't act on a vision out of fear, the greater the odds are that the vision will die in us. I was afraid that would happen to me, so even though I didn't feel like I was ready, my family and I took the leap anyway.

We really didn't know anyone in Atlanta. And really, did Atlanta need another church? You can spit and hit a steeple there. But regardless of its public image, metro Atlanta is not the buckle of the Bible Belt anymore. Most churches are not growing there. Statistics show that like most regions, most people don't attend church regularly there.[1] Our family knocked on countless doors and talked to hundreds of people in order to see if this was true.

And what did we find out? Why don't most people attend church there anymore? We were told it was because church was "boring," "hypocritical," "stuffy," "irrelevant," "out of touch," "all about money," "a big show," and many other unflattering things. Sad to say, I felt like many of these accusations were fair.

As in most places, churches face an uphill battle in metro Atlanta. Most church growth is down to churches simply swapping sheep. Every pastor I know would admit that most churches in the area have lost their way. They have gotten off track. They have forgotten why they exist. Philosophically, culturally, and ecclesiologically, most churches there are not poised to reach the hundreds of thousands of people moving to metro Atlanta from all over the world each year.

For one thing, the majority of people moving there don't understand the Christian subculture that's been created in the South. And so, they don't understand what's going on in many of the churches. Many of them weren't raised hearing the common Bible stories, and don't know many of the things churches in the South tend to consider common knowledge. People who didn't grow up in the Bible Belt a generation ago find it hard to grasp how church culture was part of everyday life then, complete with church suppers, tent revivals, and church meetings at least three times a week: Sunday morning, Sunday night, and of course, Wednesday night! People who are disconnected from Christ and the church aren't familiar with the "Christianese" language Christians often throw around. Most people don't know what it means to be "saved," much less be "washed in the blood." And they don't arrive with positive perceptions of Christians or churches. People are not interested in conforming to the old religious traditions. They are looking for something that makes a difference in their everyday lives. For all these reasons, churches are just not winning in Atlanta, as in most places around the world. Sure, a few churches are thriving. However, one church is usually growing at the expense of another. If we're honest, churches are largely swapping sheep.

Our nation is becoming more and more unchurched. Why? Most people I meet don't necessarily have a problem with God or even Jesus. It's Christians and the church they have a tough time with. When we moved to metro Atlanta to start Mountain Lake Church, our goal was to change the way people think about church. For sixteen years, this was the dream. We didn't yet have a crystal-clear vision yet, but we had a motivation. We had a dream.

WHERE'S THE VISION?

If you are familiar with the saga of the Bible, you know that God's chosen nation, Israel, was named after a man. His original name was Jacob. The name Jacob means "deceiver," and for the first part of his life, Jacob lived up to his name. He spent the first half of his life trying to deceive, manipulate, and strategize his way to success, even stealing his brother's birthright in Genesis 25. One night, however, all that changed. The story is found in Genesis 32. Jacob found himself in a wrestling match with God (or at least a messenger from God). He wrestled all night, and Scripture tells us that during the struggle, Jacob refused to let go until God blessed him. Think about it: Jacob would not stop wrestling with God until God helped him fulfill His vision for Jacob's life! And God did bless him. Everything great in Jacob's life started with a holy wrestling match over the vision. That's powerful.

 Everything great in Jacob's life started with a holy wrestling match over the vision.

When the wrestling match was over, Jacob's life was forever marked by this event. From that point onward he walked with a limp as a reminder of that night. God also renamed Jacob, which means "deceiver," to Israel, which means "he has striven with God." Because of his willingness to wrestle with God over the vision for his life and family, Israel became the father of twelve sons, who became the twelve tribes of Israel, who became God's chosen people! Jacob simply would not let go of God until God blessed him with a clear vision, purpose, and the power to carry it out.

If we are ever going to be able to be mean about the vision, we cannot skip over the wrestling process. Everything great in our lives begins with a holy wrestling match over the vision. This will not be easy. In fact, it's plain difficult, and often painful. It should be. This wrestling match with God should change the trajectory of a person's life. It should forever shape one's character and daily schedule. It should shape one's focus and renew one's passion. That's what it did for Jacob. Jacob was never the same after wrestling down the vision. God even changed his name to reflect that fact. A new vision can and should change us dramatically. That's what it did for me.

> **A new vision can and should change us dramatically. That's what it did for me.**

Before Mountain Lake's public launch in January 2000, I spent months wrestling with the vision God would have for our church. I remember sitting at my dining room table (I didn't own a desk, much less an office at the time), with my Bible and other books open, when I looked up and said these words out loud: "Belong. Become." These two words would form the core of our mission as it still stands today. Our mission soon became "Giving people a place to *belong* in a healthy relationship with God and others; *become* more like Jesus; and *bless* our world."

Keep this in mind: We didn't invent our vision. It came straight out of this cool book called the Bible! None of us actually invents the vision for our lives, churches, and organizations. We were created by God for His purposes, so we discover God's vision for our lives through our relationship with Him. If we try to go off by ourselves and invent the vision, we will make a mess of things. So how do we get the vision from God? Start with the Bible. There's a reason they call it God's Word.

In the Bible, the two most important commands are what we've come to call the Great Commandment and the Great Commission. In the Great Commandment, God reiterated through Jesus what He had said earlier in the Ten Commandments:

Jesus replied: "'Love the Lord your God with all your heart and with all your soul and with all your mind.' This is the first and greatest commandment. And the second is like it: 'Love your neighbor as yourself.' All the Law and the Prophets hang on these two commandments." (Matt. 22:37–40)

The Bible is clear that the overarching vision for our lives should be driven by love: loving God and loving others as much as we love ourselves. God desires that we belong in a healthy relationship with Him and healthy relationships with others. He wants us to be driven by our desire to please Him and serve others. The more we love and serve others, the more we look like Jesus. That's God's goal for all of our lives. It's a simple vision isn't it? Love and serve God. Love and serve people. Love is the foundation for every vision.

Later, Jesus commissioned His disciples to take His vision of love and grace and share it with everyone else in the world. We have come to call this the Great Commission:

"Therefore go and make disciples of all nations, baptizing them in the name of the Father and of the Son and of the Holy Spirit, and teaching them to obey everything I have commanded you. And surely I am with you always, to the very end of the age." (Matt. 28:19–20)

Regardless of who we are, how old we are, where we live, or what we do, God's vision for all of our lives is the same in these three important ways: (1) love and serve Him, (2) love and serve others, and (3) share the good news. When we adopted belonging, becoming, and blessing at Mountain Lake, we didn't invent this vision. We discovered it in God's Word.

A TRUE ORIGINAL

Though this overarching vision from God applies to all of us, we can still apply it to our lives in an incredibly personal way—as if it were dreamed up especially for us. While there are many common threads to the ways God calls us to serve Him, there are also unique personal and cultural contexts and nuances applied to every vision, depending on the person, the place, and the situation. It's as unique as a fingerprint. None of us has exactly the same vision that Jacob did. Your vision will not be exactly the same as mine. In fact, whatever you do, don't try to copy someone's vision! In my previous book for pastors, *The Measure of Our Success: An Impassioned Plea to Pastors*, I talk about the problem with copycat churches and every pastor's tendency to copy another church's vision. When we're unsure of our own vision, or insecure in our own leadership, it's tempting to try to copy someone else's vision. What many churches end up with is a cheap imitation.

Do you know what a knockoff is? It's an unauthorized copy or cheap imitation of the original. And for years, I'll admit, I was a knockoff junkie. I will confess to you that I have contributed to the counterfeit goods problem in our country. I love New York, and every time I would visit, I would make my way to Canal Street or Chinatown where street-side vendors and merchants were selling "Gucci" handbags, fake Rolex watches, fake Montblanc pens, and knockoffs of everything you could imagine. They even had fake Nikes!

For years, I would come home from New York with multiple knockoff products, so pleased with myself that I had gotten a product exactly like the original at a fraction of the price. I was so proud of myself—for a few weeks. You guessed it; before long those watches would stop, pens would break (or worse yet, leak ink all over the place), and the word *Gucci* would peel off my wife's purse. I began to realize that a copy is no substitute for the original. There's only one Gucci. There's only one Rolex. There's only one Montblanc. Their quality cannot be matched or imitated. That's why they those products are so desirable in the first place.

So it is with vision. An original is soon discernable from an imitation. Too many people and organizations today are getting their visions from someone else's website, blog, tweets, marketing materials, or conferences. While there's nothing wrong with being inspired by others or learning from others, there is a problem with copying a preexisting vision: we simply won't protect a knockoff—a vision that's not ours. Don't rip off someone else's vision. God has something better—much more authentic—that's meant just for you.

> Don't rip off someone else's vision. God
> has something better—much more
> authentic—that's meant just for you.

While I was lead pastor of Mountain Lake, I would get a call from another pastor from time to time, and the conversation would go like this: "Shawn, we're launching a new church. I love your mission statement there at Mountain Lake, and I just wanted permission to use it as the mission statement for our church." Every time I was asked that, I responded with an emphatic "No." Why?

Because I believe you can't skip your personal wrestling-with-God process to discover your unique mission. If you skip that critical step and substitute someone else's vision, you will question your mission at some point in the future. You will doubt it. You won't defend it when it is challenged. You can't be mean about a vision that isn't your vision. Suffice it to say, these phone conversations are usually painful and short ones, but I know this approach helps leaders in the long run. The most important thing they can do is wrestle with God until His vision for their lives and organizations becomes clear to them. To be mean about the vision, we must believe that God has uniquely revealed it to us.

Do you know what your vision is? If you have a vision, where did it come from? Do you believe God revealed it to you, did you make it up, or did you rip it off from someone or somewhere else? My prayer for all of us is that we would wrestle with God until He gives His vision specifically to us and for us.

HOLY DISCONTENT

Has God ever broken into your life and created such a sense of holy discontent that you could not help but respond to a need? Have you ever lost sleep at night because some things just aren't right in the world? Because something's missing? And here's another question: Do you know God's purpose for your life? It's probably connected to that holy discontent. If you don't know or have never experienced this, why not try asking God? Be willing to wrestle with God until He blesses you and reveals His vision for your life, and you'll reap the reward of this knowledge. If you've never had the terrible privilege of wrestling with God over a vision, know that it's far too valuable to skip over!

> If you've never had the terrible privilege of wrestling with God over a vision, know that it's far too valuable to skip over!

When I first struggled with God for our vision, I was twenty-eight years old and serving on staff at a traditional megachurch in Birmingham, Alabama. I loved my church. But for some reason, I began to struggle. I began to feel a tension surrounding me, and to envision a church culture different from the one I then served in. I began to wonder what it might look like to create an environment where nonreligious people might better fit in. In the church where I served, most people had been in church their entire lives. They knew the language. They knew the stories. They understood the traditions and the culture, so the church was great for them. But I felt that there was another large group of people in town who didn't know the stories. They weren't religious people. They didn't talk or dress or act like we did. When my unchurched friends would visit our church, they often felt out of place. They felt like they couldn't relate to the guy on the stage.

I respected our senior leader very much. But I began to realize that God was giving me a new picture of what church could look like. This didn't mean the pastor of my current church was wrong and I was right. It just meant we had two different visions for the church. I realized at a certain point that I couldn't stay there.

I remember where I was the day it happened. I was standing in the doorway between the den and the kitchen—when I felt God speak to me. Now before you think it's about to get weird, I've never heard God speak to me in an audible voice. I've never been struck with lightning, and I've never seen God write on a wall. I wish He would, but He hasn't done that for me. On this day, though, I believe He did speak—and I listened.

I was leaning against the doorway, privately thinking about the situation in my church and ministry, when I just sensed God say to me: *Shawn, if you can't support this pastor's vision 100 percent, you don't need to be here. If you stay here, and you're not completely behind the vision, then you become part of the problem. Besides, if you feel like church could be done in a more effective way and you don't go do it, then you're being disobedient to Me.*

At least it went something like that. I didn't hear it with my ears, but I got the point! I began to pray about how I could start a church that would change the way people thought about church. I resigned a few months later to move to Cumming, Georgia, and start Mountain Lake Church.

I talk to leaders all the time who sit in the second or third chair on the leadership team in their organizations. They will say something like: "The senior leader and I just aren't on the same page. What do you think I should do?" My answer is a simple one. If you can't support the vision 100 percent, you need to have the integrity to leave. It's that simple. I have never understood how an employee will accept paycheck after paycheck from an organization for years and yet consistently criticize the organization and its leaders! I'm sorry, but that lacks integrity, my friend. We don't have to agree with every single one of our organization's decisions, but we do have to agree completely with the vision. We just don't have time to debate the vision.

In my case, the moment I couldn't fully support my leader's vision, I needed to go. I wrestled with God on the issue until He spoke to me, and I listened and obeyed His command to go and start a new church. My life has never been the same because of it. If you obey God to go and start work on the new vision He gives you, your life will never be the same either.

Perhaps God can use my experience to speak to you where you're living today. Are you restless? Are you discontent about the current state of affairs? If you are not the senior leader in your organization, do you share the vision of your organization 100 percent? If not, you need to either check yourself and realign yourself with the vision of the organization—or leave. The vision is just too important for all of us not to be on the same page. We can have some different opinions, but we can't waffle on the vision. I know this sounds strong, but I will say it again: we just don't have time to debate the vision.

Maybe you need permission today to go and pursue the vision God is placing on your heart. Maybe God is speaking. You just need the courage to listen and obey. Everything begins with a clear vision from God given to a leader. It always has.

GOD SPEAKS

If you think about it, from the very beginning of time, everything has begun with God speaking His vision for us. God said "Let there be light," and there was light (Gen. 1)! God had a vision for our universe and our world—for humankind and the kind of relationship He wanted to have with us. God spoke the vision out loud.

Later on, God appointed prophets who would listen for His voice and write down what He said. Today, the Bible is God's primary way of revealing His wisdom and His plan to you and me. In His Word, God gives us the clearest and most specific advice about vision. He speaks to us about not only the importance of vision, but the source of vision. Through Solomon, the wisest man who ever lived, God said: "Where there is no vision, the people perish" (Prov. 29:18 KJV).

The word *vision* is actually best translated *revelation*. The New International Version of the Bible translates this verse even more literally from the original Hebrew: "Where there is no revelation, the people cast off restraint." In other words, where there is no vision, people run wild. People go their own way. Everyone wanders off in his or her own direction. There's no harmony. There's no common purpose, unity, or synergy. On the flip side, when God has spoken and everyone believes in the vision, there is harmony. There is common purpose, unity, and synergy!

What happens if we don't take the time to wrestle through and discover God's true vision? We will make something up. We'll do something for the sake of doing it, and we may even accomplish something worthwhile. We may still be busy running here and there trying to be "successful," whatever that means. But without a clear, God-driven picture of success, we chase the wind. We can invent a vision or adopt one from our culture, and we may even look successful in the world's eyes. But if we have not fulfilled the vision God has for us, we have not been successful in our Creator's eyes! And if we are not successful in His eyes, we fail. (I wrote a book about that.[2])

King Solomon was the wisest man who ever lived. Through him, God said: "There is a way that appears to be right, but in the end it leads to death" (Prov. 14:12). There's a big difference between a good idea and a God idea. We had better know the difference before we run off and try to change the world. Vision is something revealed by God. And, as the Bible says, without a vision from God, we will perish—and our organizations will perish along with us.

> There's a big difference between a good idea and a God idea. We had better know the difference before we run off and try to change the world.

God also tells us that where there is no vision we "cast off restraint" (Prov. 29:18). In other words, we will all wander off in our own random directions with our good ideas. We will have an absolute mess on our hands. If we don't understand the vision God has for our lives, we will drift through life, pursuing whatever catches our eye, and bouncing from one shiny and attractive thing to another. Without the guidelines, the "restraint" of a clearly defined goal, everyone will be pulling different directions. As leaders, we must be headed in a clear, consistent direction before anyone will go with us.

Our vision serves as our compass—our true north on our journey. Better than that, it comes with a Guide. We don't have to make things up and scrape along, limping after a weak or second-hand vision. God knows what He wants for us, and He wants to reveal it to us. Are you willing to wrestle with Him until He gives it to you and then have the faith to jump?

In My Journal

▶ What is God's vision for me? Have I wrestled with God until it has become crystal clear?

▶ If not, how can I pray until this happens?

▶ What does success look like for me? Why?

▶ What is the difference between a good idea and a God idea?

THREE

VISION AND SUCCESS

I truly believe that any organization can be successful if three key points are in place: if an organization's vision is clear, if it is compelling, and if there is consistency over time. Put another way:

Success = Clear Vision + Compelling
Communication + Consistent Direction

This means that vision is the deal breaker or deal maker! In his book *Built to Last*, Jim Collins discusses research findings on the principles that allow companies to be successful over the long haul. His research shatters many of the common myths about what makes organizations successful over time.[1] I want to take just a minute to highlight his findings, but then apply my own experience in debunking these myths.

MYTH: "IT TAKES A GREAT NEW IDEA TO START A GREAT COMPANY."

Built to Last: Jim and his team found that in reality, many successful organizations began with no innovative product or original idea. While they tried not to copy others, they were not above learning from others. In some cases they actually took someone else's idea and made it better. The authenticity of their vision was field-tested by their commitment: they were willing to stick with the idea over a longer period of time, while most of the other companies moved on to something new. They were committed to seeing the vision become a reality over time. Like the parable of the tortoise and the hare, visionary companies often get off to a slow start, but win the long race.[2]

My Experience: As a lead pastor and leadership consultant to thousands over the last sixteen years, I can tell you that churches have a very unique challenge when it comes to vision. The visions for all churches come out of the same book! So it's impossible to have a completely "new" vision. The Bible even says it: "There is nothing new under the sun" (Eccl. 1:9). Frankly, we shouldn't worry so much about concocting something new and exciting. God's vision for the church is already compelling. What we need is the wisdom to contextualize the vision for our environment, culture, and the people we're trying to reach. That's really the hard work of vision, as we discussed in the previous chapter.

Sure, there's a product now and again like the iPhone that comes along and blows everyone away. But even Apple didn't have revolutionary ideas or products right out of the gate. Have you ever heard of the Lisa computer? Probably not. It was a complete flop, selling only 10,000 units.[3] But it taught them a lesson. In contrast to IBM, Apple decided to simply get consumers to view their technology through an emotional and creative lens.

Most leaders in organizations I know haven't achieved success through a silver bullet—one clever new idea that no one has ever thought of before. They just made an idea better. In ministry world, however, I have watched pastors and churches jump from new idea to new idea, from new program to new program, trying to solve their church's issues. This approach never works. If one more program were going to fix the church, it would already be fixed! Most of us don't need to invent a new program or new product to be successful. What we need is one compelling, clear, and consistent vision.

MYTH: "VISIONARY COMPANIES REQUIRE GREAT, CHARISMATIC, VISIONARY LEADERS."

Built to Last: In their research, Jim and his team found that charismatic leadership is not always required to be a great leader. In fact, it could prove to be detrimental to a company's long-term prospects. Sometimes leaders are so visionary they run off and leave the very people who are responsible for making the vision happen! Some visionary leaders cast a compelling vision but never put in the work to see the vision through. Jim Collins asserts that the best leaders concentrate more on "architecting" an enduring institution over time, rather than simply relying on their own charismatic personalities to keep everything propped up. Jim calls this type of leader a Level 5 Leader. A Level 5 Leader is one who doesn't have to be the most charismatic person in the room. Instead he or she focuses on building a consistent vision that people can trust and rely on over time.[4]

My Experience: When it comes to vision, talk is cheap. Everyone has a big vision these days. The leaders who impress me are the ones who not only have a big vision but have a plan for implementing it. It's one thing to stand up and charismatically cast an inspiring vision to the crowd. It is quite another to get down in the trenches and help to drill the vision down into every level of an organization. It's one thing to have a vision. It's another thing to have a plan to accomplish it. Level 5 Leaders may not always be the most charismatic, but they have a concrete to-do list for making the vision a reality. That's what matters.

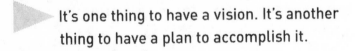

It's one thing to have a vision. It's another thing to have a plan to accomplish it.

MYTH: "VISIONARY COMPANIES SHARE A COMMON SUBSET OF 'CORRECT' CORE VALUES."

Built to Last: Jim and his team looked to see if there was a common set of values that every great organization had in common. Their research revealed, however, that no such monster existed. Among the best companies in their study, there was no "right" set of core values that they all shared. The crucial variable was not the content of a company's values, but how deeply they believed their values and how consistently they lived, breathed, and expressed them in all that they did.[5]

My Experience: Our ministry team at Mountain Lake had a set of team values. We called them "the Code." (We'll talk about the Code more in detail later.) However, these values wouldn't be worth the paper they were written on if we didn't hold ourselves accountable to living them. Clever values don't create culture. Consistent ones do. What we value is important, but how deeply we value and hold to it is more important.

MYTH: "VISIONARY COMPANIES ARE GREAT PLACES TO WORK, FOR EVERYONE."

Built to Last: Jim and his team first thought that the most effective organizations would have very low turnover compared to other companies. In reality, the greatest organizations had a great deal of turnover. In fact, only those who "fit" extremely well with the core values and demanding standards of a visionary company found these great companies great places to work. Many, however, could not make the adjustment from other cultures of status quo, and were spit out of these great companies quickly. In a great organization, employees either didn't last long, or tended to be "lifers." He stated: "If you go to work at a visionary company, you will either fit and flourish—probably couldn't be happier—or you will likely be expunged like a virus. It's binary. There's no middle ground. It's almost cultlike. Visionary companies are so clear about what they stand for and what they're trying to achieve that they simply don't have room for those unwilling or unable to fit their exacting standards."[6]

My Experience: At Mountain Lake Church, an incredible community culture ensures staff and church health. Every staff member we ever had from another church said our culture was unlike any church they have ever worked for. But that also means it always required some adjustment for new employees who were used to things like "ministry silos," where everyone stays in their designated area and no one knows or cares what anyone else on staff is doing. That is not the way to roll! Mountain Lake continues to be a *team* not a *staff*, and everyone is in each other's business. The staff constantly debriefs and even critiques each other's ministry areas to make each other better. That requires a trust and humility that many seem to struggle with. Everyone wants the privilege of being part of a team. Few want to pay the price of being on a team. Being part of a team has required a huge adjustment for many of our new staff members. Some embraced this difference after a year or so of learning how to accept critique and coaching from their peers. Others never did. Great organizations have turnover like anyone else, but most of it is desired turnover. Most people fire themselves and do so quickly when they realize they don't fit the unique culture of a great organization.

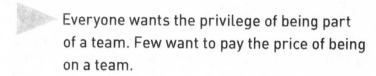 Everyone wants the privilege of being part of a team. Few want to pay the price of being on a team.

MYTH: "THE MOST SUCCESSFUL COMPANIES FOCUS PRIMARILY ON BEATING THE COMPETITION."

Built to Last: Jim and his team thought that great companies might have more of a competitive edge. Not so. In reality, visionary companies focused primarily on beating themselves. "How can we improve ourselves to do better tomorrow than we did today?" They never thought they were "good enough." They rarely compared themselves to or tried to copy other companies. They focused on being the best *them* they could be.[7]

My Experience: At Mountain Lake, we rarely talked about what another church was doing. Folks were not worried about keeping up with the other churches. We realized we were not in a race against someone else! Especially when it comes to churches, we're all on the same team. So Mountain Lake decided from the get-go to focus on constantly working on its own processes and systems. The focus is on blocking and tackling rather than the scoreboard. Great organizations tend to be more focused on the process than product. They concentrate on the fundamentals of building a great company and allow the results to take care of themselves; and they usually do.

Which of these myths have you bought into? Come on, be honest. Look back over the list. Have we believed somehow that we could be successful with or without a clear, consistent vision? Have we sold ourselves short because of lack of charismatic ability? Have we been running around looking for something new, when what we really need is to dust off the old?

Both research and experience prove it: Vision is the most important thing. Vision is everything. Wherever there is a compelling vision and clarity and consistency are applied over time, success will follow. Where there is no vision, there is no success. If you find yourself and your organization stuck today, dust off the vision, and ask yourself some key questions:

- Why does the vision matter?
- Why should other people give their lives to it?
- What is urgent about it?
- Is it compelling?
- Is it clear to everyone in the organization?
- Have we been consistent in our direction and communication?

These are questions we can't just skim over. They are life and death for us. If people don't get the vision, it's lights out! If we want new growth in our lives, families, and organizations, the vision is where it's at.

Vision is simply the most important thing in the world. Where there is no vision, remember, the people perish and cast off restraint! Without vision, there is no compelling reason to take the next hill. "Beating the competition" will not suffice for a vision. Neither will satisfying everyone, having a snappy new attraction, or even growing.

If we give in to the myths above, we will spend our days trying to fix things that won't fix things. We will waste our days and our energy trying to make things better, only to realize our work has been futile.

On the flip side, think about it: Isn't it encouraging to know that we don't need to have a revolutionary idea that no one has ever thought of to be successful? Isn't it encouraging to know that we don't have to be the best communicator or charismatic leader in the world? Isn't it encouraging to be reminded that we don't have to do it like someone else is doing it? Isn't it encouraging to know that people leave because of the vision not just in the absence of one? Everything rises and falls on vision. If we get that right, and we stick to it, everything else is secondary.

In My Journal

▸ What myth about vision have I tended to buy into?

▸ What do I need to do to debunk this myth in our organization?

▸ What is the most encouraging truth about these myths?

FOUR

A VISION WE'RE WILLING TO DIE FOR

It sounds dramatic, but let me ask you a question: Would you be willing to die for your vision? If not, please don't skip this chapter. You're probably not ready for the rest of this book. Why? If your vision ever has a chance of becoming a reality, it must be such deep-seated moral conviction that you're willing to do anything to see it through. You must believe the vision is even bigger than you. As leaders we need to know that at some point in the future, we will be asked to risk everything for the vision. Roll the dice. Bet the farm. Sacrifice it all. The vision must be that important.

To discover a vision we're willing to die for, we should first believe that God has revealed His unique purpose for our lives and the organizations we lead. As we discussed at the beginning of this book, we must believe God has given the vision to us to steward well. If we believe that God has spoken to us and called us to something more significant than ourselves, it will be easier when we're asked to sacrifice for it. Our willingness to do that will ultimately determine whether we are successful.

If God has spoken to us and revealed a specific direction for our lives and organizations, it is a scary but powerful thing! All of a sudden, it's not about us anymore. We have a higher calling and purpose. We have a higher level of determination. We are more resolved to see it through. We are unwilling to waver. We're unlikely to quit when it gets difficult. And it will get difficult! If God has given us a vision, and we quit on it, we're being disobedient to God. If we allow someone to hijack the vision, we've allowed someone else to make us disobedient to God. We'll talk more about difficulties and pitfalls later on. But for now let me say, your vision should be deep enough to withstand it all.

You've already heard about the dangers and disappointments of copying a vision. But there's something more that will help you avoid that pitfall: God has *already* made you unique, and all that's left to do is find how that plays out in your vision.

My friend Will Mancini wrote a great book a few years back entitled *Church Unique* that speaks to the cookie-cutter visions many churches tend to have these days. This comes from "modeling themselves" after a certain church. The public successes of many of today's megachurches create a great temptation for other churches to try to copy them.[1] And it's easy to see why. But Mancini suggests that instead of trying to copy a certain style or model of church, each church should instead identify its own "Kingdom Concept." The Kingdom Concept is the "simple, clear, big idea that defines how a church will glorify God and make disciples."[2]

Mancini goes on to say:

Your Kingdom Concept is what differentiates you from every other church in how you develop followers of Christ for God's ultimate honor. The Kingdom Concept answers important questions such as "What is our greatest opportunity to have an impact on the kingdom?" and "What can we do better than ten thousand other churches?"[3]

I believe that every organization needs a Kingdom Concept. Every organization should seek something that it can do better than every other organization. When we understand our Kingdom Concept, it breeds passion, determination, and tenacity. Doing the hard work up front—and laying hold of a unique vision in a deep way—will give us a vision worth dying for.

Think about this. God created every one of us uniquely. There never has been, nor will there ever be, anyone just like you. Your one-of-a-kind DNA proves it. Why do you think God created us this way? We have a unique role to play in His plan! When God speaks to us, He specifically tailors our role in His vision based on how we are wired and gifted. God knows us intimately and values us as individuals. King David understood this about his own leadership:

> For you created my inmost being;
>   you knit me together in my mother's womb.
> I praise you because I am fearfully and wonderfully made;
>   your works are wonderful,

> *I know that full well.*
> *My frame was not hidden from you*
>> *when I was made in the secret place,*
>> *when I was woven together in the depths of the earth.*
> *Your eyes saw my unformed body;*
>> *all the days ordained for me were written in your book*
>> *before one of them came to be.*
>
> (Ps. 139:13–16)

Here's my question: If God created us this uniquely and knows us this intimately, down to the number of hairs on our heads (easier for some than others), and He formed His plan for us before we were born, why are we trying to be like someone else? Why do we have a copycat vision? Why are we trying to keep up with the Joneses? Who are they anyway? God has wired us the way we're wired for a reason. He has raised us up in this generation for this time and this place. He has a purpose for us to fulfill.

Thousands of years after King David lived and died, Luke, the author of the book of Acts, said this about him: "Now when David had served God's purpose in his own generation, he fell asleep; he was buried with his ancestors and his body decayed" (Acts 13:36). What a way to sum up a life! We all have just one life to live. We only have a few short years to live it. We'll all soon decay. In the meantime, God has put us here for a purpose! That's where we get a vision worth living *and* dying for. When God uniquely wired us with the gifts we have, gave us the experiences we've had, and entrusted us with our resources, He did it so we might turn around and offer it all to Him to be a part of His plan.

OUR GREATEST RESPONSIBILITY

John Maxwell, *New York Times* bestselling author on leadership, has said "leadership is influence."[4] This means that whether we are in the top bubble on our organization's chart or not, if we have influence, we are leaders. This influence is a sacred trust; leaders can squander it, lose it, or leverage it to accomplish the vision God has for us.

When most of us think of the word *stewardship* we usually think about money. But the word *steward* simply means manager, as opposed to owner. Remember: we don't actually own anything. God owns it all. God entrusts everything we have to us for us to manage for His purposes. He expects us to manage everything well and use it to accomplish the vision He has for us. That vision, and the people God has entrusted to us to accomplish it, is our greatest stewardship responsibility. God is counting on us to be good stewards. It doesn't matter how big or small the vision is; our responsibility is the same. Being mean about the vision is a stewardship decision.

In the gospel of Matthew, Jesus tells the parable of the talents. In this parable, the owner of an estate goes away on a trip. Before leaving, the owner (who symbolizes Jesus, by the way) gives three different servants three different levels of "talents" to manage for him while he is away. In Jesus' day a talent was a large unit of money. The owner gives one servant five talents. He gives the other servant two talents, and the final servant one talent. Their responsibility, however, regardless of what they have been given, is the same. They are each to manage well whatever they've been given. The first two servants manage their talents efficiently and effectively. The owner responds by saying, "Well done, good and faithful servant. You have been faithful over a little; I will set you over much. Enter into the joy of your master" (Matt. 25:21 ESV).

The third servant, however, does not do the same. Motivated by fear, he decides to go and bury his talent. The owner responds by saying, "So take the talent from him and give it to him who has the ten talents. For to everyone who has will more be given, and he will have an abundance. But from the one who has not, even what he has will be taken away" (Matt. 25:28–29 ESV).

The point of Jesus' parable becomes pretty clear when applied to the vision that God has given us. It doesn't matter how big or small our vision is. Our responsibility is the same. We steward well whatever we've been given. We not only need to protect it; we need to grow it, multiply it, and honor our Master with it. Stewarding the vision well is one of the most important ways to honor God.

When I was a kid I collected Hot Wheels. I had over fifty by the time I outgrew them. But I held on to them so I could one day pass them down to my kids. Years later, I finally surprised my son by giving my entire collection to him on his birthday. I told him that these were a big deal to me, and that one day he could pass them down to his son. I told him to take care of them, be careful not to lose them, and never, ever give them away. Like most boys, he forgot everything I told him. A few years later, he and his mom were cleaning out his closet and decided to give all of his old toys away, *including* his collection of Hot Wheels. I found out about it later. It may sound silly to you, but this was a big deal to me! My family had some "intense fellowship" over that one. I couldn't believe my son would give away a gift that meant so much to me when I gave it to him!

Don't you see? This is the way God feels when He entrusts a vision to us, and we squander it, lose it, or give it away. The gifts we have and our vision may not seem like much to us, but it's everything to God. He gave it to us with great desires for the future.

I was a twenty-eight-year-old kid from Alabama who spoke with a slow, Southern drawl. I had never taught regularly to adults! When I began to share my dream to reach thousands in metro Atlanta, I had some tell me I should shrink down my dream to something more doable. I'm glad I didn't listen to the dream killers. You shouldn't either. Don't listen to people who tell you the dream is too big. If you do, your dream will not only die; you will die slowly on the inside as well. You may or may not be successful with your dream, but you must try. You have what it takes because God put this vision in you! What you have may not seem like much to you, but it is all God needs to accomplish His vision through you. All of this is why you absolutely must get and stay focused on this vision.

THE POWER OF FOCUS

I was an athlete in high school. I was fairly quick and agile (if I do say so myself), so I could play just about any sport at a reasonably high level. I played some basketball and baseball, but football was my sweet spot. Football was my passion. I lived and breathed it. I played tight end and cornerback. I loved to run (I'm proud of my fastest forty-yard dash time: 4.65). I even loved to hit people (in legal ways). There was a season in my life when I focused fifty-two weeks a year on becoming the best tight end in our state. While other athletes played basketball, baseball, lacrosse, and track, I decided to focus solely on becoming a one-sport star. I eventually made All-County and All-Region. I even received a few scholarship offers from smaller schools, but decided to take another route in my life (honestly, you would never have heard of me if I hadn't). Effort and passion will only take you so far. Focus took me further than I could have gone any other way.

Most sports require intense focus for success. There are only a few select athletes in history who have succeeded at the highest levels playing multiple sports: for instance Bo Jackson excelled at both baseball and football. But "Prime Time" Deion Sanders (known more for his touchdown dances) and Michael Jordan couldn't even be successful in multiple sports! Even if athletes play multiple sports in high school, most college coaches will press them to focus on one sport by the time they get to college. Why? Most coaches know that in the long run, you can't be great at everything.

Did you know this is true for the organizations we lead? We can't be successful at everything. We won't win if we try to do everything. One of the most common mistakes organizations make is trying to do too much. We try to be all things to all people. We launch too many programs and too many products, hoping that will attract people and keep them. But the world of athletics reminds us we can't be great at everything. The best way to be great is to be great at one thing.

What does your organization have the potential to be the best in the world at? To get there, you have some very tough decisions ahead of you. As the vision becomes clearer, it will be just as important that you decide what *not* to do as it will be what you're going to do. You cannot be all things to all people. You're not going to reach everyone. You're not great at everything, but you can become great at one thing. That's good news! To be successful, we only need to become experts at one thing. The less we do, the greater our odds of success.

Our focus will largely determine the level of our success. Talent is not enough. Busyness does not equal effectiveness. Discipline and focused intensity over time is where it's at. A disciplined, focused organization is an attractive organization. People want to be part of something that's headed in a clear, compelling direction. People begin to take notice. People begin to sign up. That one thing your organization does best—that unique vision worth living and dying for—that's the center of our bulls-eye. Now that we are focused, you know what our primary responsibility is every day we get up? Keep everyone else focused on the bulls-eye! This is the really hard work of leadership. Welcome to the next level. The air is thinner up here!

 Our focus will largely determine
the level of our success.

In My Journal

▶ What am I good at? What are my gifts?

▶ What can I be the best at?

▸ What one thing does my organization do better than any other?

▸ Would I die for the vision? Why or why not?

▸ What are some things my organization could benefit from *not* focusing on?

FIVE

KEEPING THE
VISION ALIVE IN ME

Bill Hybels, pastor of Willow Creek Church, was the first person I ever heard use the phrase "vision leaks."[1] When I first heard those words, I remember thinking: *Wow, does it ever!* Vision just has a way of losing steam over time. People and organizations try to do too many things. They bite off more than they can chew. They get busy. They get distracted. They lose their passion, get discouraged, and want to quit. Vision leaks! We had better recognize it and be proactive about it. So what do we do?

Let me tell you a story. My family loves the beach. I think my wife Tricia would live there if she could. By *there*, I do mean literally *on* the beach. And our kids are perfectly content playing all day on the beach every day of vacation. Especially when the kids were smaller, it wasn't enough just to carry towels, sunscreen, and snacks to the beach. We had to carry toys, including shovels and sand buckets with us. When my family goes to the beach it always looks like we're moving there permanently! My kids always loved to dig a huge hole in the sand with their shovels. Then they would make runs to the ocean with their buckets, and pour buckets of water into their homemade saltwater lake. But with each new dump, we watched as the water dissipated down through the sand. My kids weren't discouraged. They just ran to the ocean again, thinking that maybe one more trip would make the difference. Three buckets more and three minutes later, they began to realize that if they wanted to enjoy their little lake by the ocean, they were going to need to keep making water trips every three minutes, because it constantly leaked!

As leaders we pour our vision into people. We pour out our hearts into people. We cast a compelling vision at an annual retreat, an anniversary Sunday, or annual vision day. People are inspired. People are moved. They are fired up! Everyone seems to be on the same page.

Three weeks later, however, it seems as though we're back in the same place. The same old issues have bubbled up again. Things seem out of alignment. The same old frustrations show up. The natives seem restless. The vision has once again gotten dry. Were we not clear enough in our last talk? Did we not cast the vision well? Were we not convincing or compelling enough? Have they already forgotten everything we talked about? If we don't recognize that vision, by its very nature, leaks, we'll get discouraged when it does. When the vision begins to leak we'll think: *Maybe I'm just not a good leader. Maybe I'm not the right leader. Maybe I'm in the wrong place. Maybe everyone would be better if I just stepped aside.* Do you see where this is going?

The truth is that no matter how clear the vision is, no matter how convincingly we communicate it, vision will trickle out faster than the water in my kids' beach lake. It leaks faster than we think it does too. Hybels said that vision leaks every six weeks.[2] I would actually say that within the span of one month, it's easy to get distracted, forget what's important, get discouraged, and lose our way!

> Being mean about the vision requires
> consistently recasting the vision in creative ways.

As key leaders, our most important job is to keep the vision alive and intact. To do that, we'll need to consistently run back to the source of our vision, and pour it out in our organizations with great passion and fervor. Over. And over. And over.

The next time you walk down the beach, notice something. Dozens of other families have also dug their own homemade saltwater lakes, but most of them are now dry. Why? Because somewhere along the line, one member of the family grew weary of refilling the bucket. The same can happen to us when it comes to vision. How do we maintain the strength we need to keep pouring into the vision? I'm glad you asked.

IT STARTS WITH ME

Vision doesn't begin to spring a leak somewhere out there, in other people. Vision leaks first in me! I get distracted. I get disillusioned, disappointed, discouraged. I get tired. First and foremost, because

I am a leader, everyone is depending on me to maintain the passion and energy that vision requires. They're counting on me to regularly run to the source, fill up my vision bucket time and again, then challenge everyone else to keep doing the same. If I grow weary of the vision, everyone else will. If I give up on the vision, everyone else will be quick to follow. So what do we do? How can we prevent the vision from leaking rapidly in us?

Most of us have several leadership challenges and questions rolling around in our heads at any given time: *Who* can we recruit? *What* are we going to do about *this* or *them*? *Where* can we find the new leader we need? *When* should we pull the trigger on this? *How* should we address that?

Out of all the questions we must wrestle with, though, there's one question that's more important than all the others: *"Why*?" Why are we doing this? Why do we *want* to do this? Why are we dreaming what we're dreaming? Why should anyone care? Why is asking "Why?" so important? First of all, answering it reveals our motives. Often, what we think is God's dream can actually be our dream in disguise. We don't always have the purest motivations. We don't always understand our own hearts. The Bible says, "The heart is deceitful above all things, and desperately sick; who can understand it?" (Jer. 17:9 ESV).

Can I ask you a question? What's driving you? No, really. *Why* do you want to build what you're building? To be big? To be famous? To have a platform? Jesus said "For where your treasure is, there your heart will be also" (Matt. 6:21).

When it comes to vision, motivation matters. There are tons of man-made dream drivers out there: Crowds. Numbers. Buildings.

Budgets. Approval. Fame. Fortune. If we're honest, these are the things that often become the dream drivers in our organizations. In my book for Christian leaders, *The Measure of Our Success*, I talk about the havoc these man-made dream drivers have caused in my life, family, and ministry. Whenever I have forgotten *why* I do what I do, I turn into a restless, dogmatic, impatient guy who will run over people and use them to get work done. I become mean in the worst sort of way. That's Shawn Lovejoy when he's unhealthy. What about you? When you lose sight of the vision, how does it exhibit itself? Destruction? Despair? Both?

 When it comes to vision, motivation matters.

Nobody starts out this way. It just happens. Gradually. I remember the first time I woke up to realize it had happened to me. I was twenty years old when God finally got completely ahold of me. This made all the difference in my life. I can remember coming home from my college classes and reading the Bible for hours at a time. In those days I would share my faith with anyone who would listen. My friends started calling me "Apostle Shawn." I still haven't figured out if that was a compliment or not. A couple years later, I surrendered to God's call on my life to vocational ministry. By the age of twenty-eight, I had moved to Atlanta with my family to start a church. Those first two years of getting a new church off the ground turned out to be the hardest years of our lives. Things weren't great at home, either. In the early days of starting Mountain Lake Church, I allowed the whole endeavor to bury me: emotionally, relationally, spiritually, and even physically. For two years, I thought of almost nothing besides Mountain Lake Church. I mean, *nothing*. I rarely if ever took a day off. And then, finally, my work-aholism seemed to start paying off!

Two years into our new church, significant growth finally began to happen. Our church moved to a new location and doubled in size within a few weeks. For the first time in quite a while, I began to feel good about myself again. So good, in fact, that one night as my wife, Tricia, and I were lying in bed, I asked her, "Well, babe, how do you think things are going?" Have you ever asked someone something but didn't really want to know the answer? I was actually just fishing for compliments. I expected Tricia to say was something like, "Wow, Shawn, things are going great. You are the greatest pastor and leader I've ever seen. I'm so honored to be your partner." Instead, while staring at the bedroom ceiling, she answered my question with a question of her own: "Do you really want to know how I feel?" I knew I was in trouble.

Tricia began, "I don't think things are going well at all. I actu-ally think you have allowed this church to turn you into a workaholic. You're never home. You never take a day off. I'm not even sure Hannah [our then two-year-old] knows you." She continued, "When you are home, you're always tired. You have a short fuse, and you're not all that fun to be around. In fact, there's a growing part of me wishing I had the Shawn who was up on the stage every week, humorous and happy, not the one who comes home with us. I'm not sure I like the person you've become."

Now, normally, when my wife would try to play the role of the Holy Spirit in my life, I would instantly become defensive. This time, however, something miraculous happened. It was as if scales fell off my eyes immediately. I had been blind to it before, but now it was as if I could clearly see who I had become. Two years as a senior pastor and church planter, with all its unique burdens, had completely stolen my sense of joy. And as the spiritual leader of my family, I was robbing them of joy. I had not seen it, but my wife was right.

The next morning when we got up, I called my ministry partner and told him my wife and I needed to get away for a week. (We had not taken a vacation in three years.) I canceled everything on my calendar and left town with my family. Over the next seven days, Tricia and I took walks on the beach while we shouted at each other, cried with each other, prayed with each other, and shared pain with each other. Near the end of the week, we began to turn a corner. We mapped out a plan to redeem our lives, our marriage, our family, and our ministry. We put boundaries in place to limit work time and make our home a soft place to fall again. I believe that week saved my marriage—and my ministry. We turned everything around. That's why my wife likes me today!

I realized during those days that because of my unhealthy patterns, rhythms, and drives, the vision had gotten lost. I had forgotten why I was doing what I was doing. When I slowed down long enough to recover that, I gained new fuel not only for my ministry but also for every component of my life!

It took some focused attention to turn away from workaholism—and away from other habits that had been draining me. I'm sad to say that during those first two years, I don't remember opening my Bible much, other than when I was trying to figure out what to teach on Sunday. I rarely if ever opened it merely for the personal truths that had fueled the passion of that twenty-year-old kid. And that's not the only time this leakage has happened to me. It has happened many times since then. It turns out I have an amazing propensity to forget why I'm doing what I'm doing. I know I'm not the only one.

FRESH SPIRITUAL DISCIPLINES

Since those days I have realized the value of not only returning to the habits that placed me where I am now, but also retracing the experiences that led me here. First of all, to keep the vision alive in me, for me, I needed to return to the foundational spiritual disciplines of Bible reading and prayer—and in creative ways. God had to rekindle the vision in me. No one else could do it! During this time I even started journaling for the first time in my life.

I have an embarrassing confession to make: at one time, I thought journaling was something only for girls and sissies. But during those days, that changed. One day in my study time, after reading something powerful and sensing that God had just spoken to me through it, it hit me over the head like a ton of bricks: *If God ever speaks to me, I might want to write it down.* I started journaling that day. From then on, whenever I was reading Scripture or any other type of book and I sensed God might be speaking to me through something I read, I wrote it down. At the beginning of the line I would simply write, "WGS" (what God said). Looking back now through ten years of journals, I now see hundreds of lines preceded by those three golden letters. I can find statements that, in hindsight, have shaped my life. I'm reminded of truths that I have long since forgotten. And I'm reminded most importantly that God has been faithful in speaking to me and leading me all these years. He has been active in my life. I am not where I am by accident!

I also began journaling many of my prayers. I've never been formally diagnosed with Attention Deficit Disorder, but I have always been an ADD pray-er. Perhaps you've had a prayer experience similar to this: "Lord, thank you for this beautiful day . . . I guess it's going to be a beautiful day. I haven't checked the weather. I probably need to check the weather on my iPhone. Hmm. Partly cloudy. Now where was I? What was I doing?" Prayer over.

But I find that journaling my prayers has greatly increased my ability to pray in focused, specific ways. Even if when I do get distracted, because it's written down, I can come back and pick up right where I left off. Journaling my prayers helps me pray specifically and directly. It helps me solidify my thoughts by putting them into words.

Perhaps the greatest value in journaling my prayers is that I can go back and review the way my relationship with God has grown and progressed. I can view the ups and the downs, the mountaintops and the valleys. I'm reminded of the unique times in my life when I sensed God speaking directly to me. I'm reminded of prayers that were answered. Of miracles He's done in my life.

Henry Blackaby, author of *Experiencing God*, calls these "spiritual markers." A spiritual marker identifies a time of decision when we clearly knew that God has somehow guided us.[3] For Moses, the burning bush on the mountain—when he heard God speak to him—was a spiritual marker he would never forget. Most of us will never experience a burning bush, but we do need burning-bush-like spiritual markers. We need to be able to trace our lives back to a moment when we know we were called to do what we are doing.

I have often found it helpful to consistently retrace these spiritual markers in my life. Over time, I can look back and see how God has faithfully directed my life according to His divine purpose. When I review my markers, I see more clearly the directions God has moved in my life and ministry.

This helps me maintain the all-important vision. As I retrace God's activity in my life, I'm reminded why I am where I am doing what I'm currently doing.

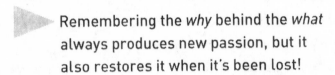

Remembering the *why* behind the *what* always produces new passion, but it also restores it when it's been lost!

REMEMBER THE PASSION

Do you remember when you felt God tapping you on the shoulder and calling you to where you are now? Do you remember when you first began the journey you are on now? Do you remember when you believed you could change the world? When life's purpose and calling was clear?

Or have you forgotten? Restoring spiritual discipline and remembering these critical moments will help you plug the vision leak in yourself. Perhaps your life and work have become more about survival and making budget. Maybe it is more about beating the competition than living out the personal mission God has given you.

If we do what we do for any other reason than out of a sense of calling for the vision, it is the wrong *why*. It's tempting to think success starts in our heads with some new strategy or system. But success starts in our hearts: "Above all else, guard your heart, for it is the wellspring of life" (Prov. 4:23 NIV 1984).

God doesn't primarily want our intellect, our leadership skills, our hard work, or even our sacrifice. He wants our hearts. He wants our vision from Him to drive everything we do. If you have ever gotten lost in all the minutia of your career and forgotten why you're doing what you're doing, you're not alone. Just look at the church at Ephesus in the New Testament for a great example. This church started out as a vibrant, passionate congregation. The apostle Paul started the church and maintained a close relationship with it for years. But evidently within one generation, they had forgotten *why* they were doing *what* they were doing. In the book of Revelation, Jesus comes along in a vision to John and calls them on the carpet. He basically says: "Guys: you are still busy doing all of the Christian activity you've been doing for years, but something's not right." Jesus said: "Yet I hold this against you: You have forsaken the love you had at first" (Rev. 2:4). They had a passion problem.

When Jesus spoke, He spoke with passion. He spoke with conviction. "The crowds were amazed at his teaching, because he taught as one who had authority, and not as their teachers of the law" (Matt. 7:28–29). When He spoke people could see in His eyes and hear in His voice something that told them He really believed what He was saying. Everything Jesus said and did flowed out of the vision God had given Him for His life and the lives of His people. Everyone could tell that.

The good news is that if we want our leadership to be attractive and powerful, we don't have to be a great expositor or eloquent communicator like Jesus was. We don't need to have some new truth or mission or strategy that no one has ever heard before. But the one thing we can't do without—as a leader or as a follower—is passion. This is why Jesus told the church at Ephesus: "Consider how far you have fallen! Repent and do the things you did at first" (Rev. 2:5). In other words Jesus said: "Go back to the practices, behaviors, and experiences that put you here in the first place. Rebuild your passion."

Take a moment to remember when you first felt the vision being birthed in you. For me, it was while teaching a college-and-career Sunday-school class at my home church when I was a twenty-two-year-old fresh out of college. I was so in love with God back then. My passion for the Lord was contagious. Because of that passion (not my intellect or skill, I assure you) that little Sunday-school class of four people exploded to more than fifty people within a year. People from all walks of life began to show up. We had everything from prostitutes to crack addicts to preachers' kids (the wildest ones) showing up every week in my class. You can be sure we rocked that little Baptist church. Some of the students were driving from thirty minutes away every week just to be a part of what God was doing in that class. A spiritual awakening spread through the whole church over the next year because of what God did there!

Meanwhile, in the midst of this volunteer ministry, I was also enjoying a successful real estate career. I made a six-figure income that year. Remember, I was only twenty-two years old. All of a sudden strange things began to happen. My involvement in that volunteer ministry was becoming more exciting and fulfilling than all the success I was having in my career. I can specifically remember one moment when I was walking out of a real estate clos-ing with a large check from the attorney in my hand, and thinking *I wish I was hanging out with some of those students right now.* Then I thought, *What's wrong with me?* It turns out nothing was wrong with me. God was doing something right in me.

Later, I remember sitting at McDonald's with some friends one Sunday after church, telling them, "Wouldn't it be cool to start a church where the whole church was filled with people like those who fill our Sunday-school class?" That conversation led to many more conversations and later confirmation that God was calling me into vocational ministry. The year I quit the real estate business, I was the top-selling agent in the county. That meant little to me though. I had been given a vision. That vision still sets the course and direction for my life today.

Do you remember when God first called you? Do you remember how passionate you were? What would it look like for you to return to that place? What would it take for you to return to the water for a new supply of vision? Before we can cast the vision to others, we have to begin with ourselves. Remembering your passion, and refreshing your spiritual discipline, will plug your personal leak. Return to the source of the vision to fill up your bucket again. Once you do, everything gets easier from there.

In My Journal

▶ Is the vision hot or cold in me? Was I ever more passionate than I am now? Why or why not?

▶ Could my pace be silently killing off the vision in me?

▶ If so, what can I do about it?

▶ How can I keep the vision alive in me on a consistent basis?

▶ Does the vision dictate my day? Or does my day dictate the vision?

SIX

KEEPING THE VISION
ALIVE IN OTHERS

Most of us overcomplicate the vision. The best thing to do, though, is to keep it simple. We ought to be able to tell someone all about it in ten seconds. The vision shouldn't be longer than a sentence. Why is this so important? No one will remember much more than a sentence. We aren't the only ones who need to remember the vision. Everyone else has to have a grasp of it too. If it is ever going to be successful, everyone needs to be able to both remember it and share it with others. A vision is only as strong as it can be shared and applied.

Having a vision is the starting point, not the finish line. Our next leadership task is to pass it on so that others can make it their own. That means the vision must be clear, compelling, and consistent. This may be one of the toughest tasks when it comes to vision.

Let me give you a bad example. I found this church mission

statement from a church near you. I've removed the church name for obvious reasons, but here it is:

> "[This church] is called to proclaim the Gospel of Christ
> and the beliefs of the evangelical Christian faith,
> to maintain the worship of God,
> and to inspire in all persons a love for Christ,
> a passion for righteousness,
> and a consciousness of their duties to God
> and their fellow human beings.
> We pledge our lives to Christ
> and covenant with each other
> to demonstrate His Spirit
> through worship, witnessing, and ministry
> to the needs of the people of this church and the community."

Now first of all, let me begin by saying that I completely agree theologically with this mission statement. That being said, if by chance you are the leader of this church, I don't mean to be embarrassing or critical; but I am about to speak the truth in love, and I hope it helps. Not one person in the church, including the pastor, could remember all of this. This mission statement is too long. As I said above, in my opinion, a mission statement should never be longer than a sentence. If the leader can't remember all of the mission, how in the world will everyone else remember it, live it, or share it? A mission will spread only to the extent it can be remembered and communicated in a clear, compelling way!

If I were writing the same mission statement, I would do

everything I could to make it more simple. I might say: "Our mission at _____ church is to *share* Christ, *move* others to follow Christ, and *model* His love in our world." Compare that with the church's statement above. It summarizes everything in the original statement. Here's the deal: If I'm lucky, I can remember about three things. If I remember them, I can do three things. If I can be successful at three things, I'm going to share that with others in a compelling way.

Where can we find a great example of clear, concise visions? Try Jesus. He made the vision simple. He boiled every command in the Bible down to two commands:

"'Love the Lord your God with all your heart and with all your soul and with all your mind.' This is the first and greatest commandment. And the second is like it: 'Love your neighbor as yourself.'" (Matt. 22:37–39)

Powerful. The religious authorities had made a relationship with God so complicated! Then Jesus came along and boiled the Christian life down to two things: loving God and loving people. Jesus simplified what mankind made complex. That's one reason why the *gospel* is good news. It's not complicated! By the way, our mission should also be good news. If our mission is only a list of dos and don'ts, it won't be attractive to people. The vision should speak to people's God-given desires for purpose and identity. It should be both short and sweet!

After reading this, you might feel that you have some chain-saw work to do on your mission statement. You don't need to *change* it, per se. But try cutting it up and refashioning it into something simple. Once this is done, you're ready to communicate it.

OVERCOMMUNICATE IT

My wife, Tricia, and I sometimes miscommunicate. Most of the time it's because she swears she told me something and I don't think she did. Bless her heart. (You know I'm kidding.) The truth is that she usually has told me. It's just that one of two things has happened: either I never heard her in the first place, or I did hear her and I've forgotten everything she told me. For these reasons, my wife will often begin our day or call me during the day and begin our phone conversation with these words: "Hey, don't forget to _____." I am always thankful for the reminder. It keeps me out of the doghouse, and off the couch. Everyone needs a gentle nudge.

In my coaching with leaders, they will often say to me: "Oh, Shawn, we remind people already. We talk about our vision all the time." But are you sure? Have you talked about it to the point that everyone knows it and can share it? Here's a test: in your next staff meeting, hand out a slip of paper and a pen to everyone. Ask everyone to write out the mission statement word for word. Give them only thirty seconds to do so. Then take up the sheets and review them. Prepare to be discouraged. The purpose of this exercise is not to embarrass people. The fact is, if everyone doesn't know the vision, it's usually not their fault. Something's usually missing in the leader's communication.

Other people often don't know the vision as well as we think they do. You may not have been as clear as you think you have. Are you ever the butt of jokes for talking about the vision too much? If so, you're probably getting *close* to saying it enough. We must refuse to stop talking about the vision until it completely saturates every person in every corner of our organization! When everyone knows the vision, is compelled by it, and contagiously shares it with others, the vision becomes unstoppable.

Multiple Mission Moments

For years at Mountain Lake Church where I pastored, the purpose of the welcome time during each service was both to greet our guests *and* to communicate the vision clearly over and over again. We confined those moments to just three minutes total, or one hundred and eighty seconds. Those three minutes were three of the most important minutes in each service, and I would never let anyone forget it. Every week, one of our pastors would take the stage at some point near the front end of the service and say something like this:

> "Hey, I'm one of the pastors here at Mountain Lake. I want to welcome you to our church. In case you don't know it, our church is on a mission. Our mission is giving people a place to *belong* in a healthy relationship with God and others, *become* more like Jesus, and *bless* our world. We would love for you to become part of our mission. In the meantime, we hope you experience that mission being lived out by our church today. It's going to be a great weekend here. We'll continue the service in a moment,

but before we do that, we are a place to *belong*, so would you be willing to get out of your comfort zone, stand up, turn around, high-five someone, and say, 'Welcome home!'"

In less than three minutes we reminded everyone in the entire organization why we existed—why we're together. We let every new person know what our church was all about. We clarified the win for the day, and rallied everyone around the mission. Then, immediately, we put the vision into practice. We made an intentional effort to help people feel like they belonged. All in less than three minutes! Remember, we did this almost every week, fifty-two times a year. It would be hard *not* to remember the vision after all that.

Leaders must figure out how to have multiple "mission moments" consistently in their organizations. These moments need to be planned. They need to be intentional. They need to be consistent and systematized. In just three minutes every week, you too can rally the troops, raise morale, and refocus everyone. Carve out a few minutes in your weekly talk. Circle up the staff. Utilize technology. Send out an email or video. Give it some thought: When, where, and how often do you need multiple mission moments? How could you create them? How could you establish consistency with them? These mission moments are like buckets full of water, refilling the vision proactively.

Make It Visual; Keep It in Front of Them

Visual tools and branding elements also allow us to keep the vision in front of people as much as possible. If done well, the sign out front, the signs in the lobby, the worship guides, even T-shirts, drink tumblers, and gel bracelets all should remind people about the vision.

Whatever it may look like for you, being mean about the vision requires consistently keeping it in front of people: both verbally and visually.

How are you keeping the vision in front of people? How often do you talk about it? Where can it be displayed? Is it memorable? Is it visual? Does everyone understand how each element of your organization fits into the whole? Communicating this in every way possible is one of our greatest leadership tasks.

ORIENT THE NEWBIES

The best time for someone to understand and embrace the mission is from the very beginning. The vision is less likely to spring a leak when you know the vessel is strong from the outset. When new staff members joined our team at Mountain Lake, the first thing we did was introduce them to our mission. We asked them to memorize the mission statement the first week they were there. We spent a lot of time talking about values as a staff. You might remember that we called our set of team values "the Code." Here's how that breaks down:

THE CODE

Community: *We love and do life with each other.*
"Dear friends, since God loved us that much, we surely ought to love each other." (1 John 4:11 NLT)

Honesty: *We speak the truth in love.*

"As iron sharpens iron, so a friend sharpens a friend."
(Prov. 27:17 NLT)

Teamwork: *We work together.*

"He makes the whole body fit together perfectly. As each
part does its own special work, it helps the other parts
grow, so that the whole body is healthy and growing and
full of love." (Eph. 4:16 NLT)

Loyalty: *We protect and honor each other.*

"You who are younger must accept the authority of the
elders. And all of you, dress yourselves in humility, for
'God opposes the proud but gives grace to the humble.'"
(1 Pet. 5:5 NLT)

Resourcefulness: *We honor God with what we have.*

"And whatever you do or say, do it as a representative
of the Lord Jesus, giving thanks through him to God the
Father." (Col. 3:17 NLT)

Execution: *We do what we say we will do.*

"Just say a simple, 'Yes, I will,' or 'No, I won't.' Anything
beyond this is from the evil one." (Matt. 5:37 NLT)

Sacrifice: *We're willing to pay the price.*

"Work willingly at whatever you do, as though you were
working for the Lord rather than for people." (Col. 3:23 NLT)

We told our new ministry team members (and then reminded everyone else constantly) that if anyone ever got fired from our ministry team, it wouldn't be for making a mistake. It would be for violating the Code. In more than twenty years of vocational ministry, I fired only three people. All three of them were fired for violating our values. That's being mean about the vision.

I'm aware of the fact that most teams have a set of values. However, there's a difference between aspirational values and realized values. Most organizations have values they aspire to, but they don't always *happen* consistently. I feel incredibly blessed that I can say with integrity that values at Mountain Lake were realized. They happened. We saw to it!

> There's a difference between
> aspirational values and realized values.
> One is a dream. One gets done.

The sooner newbies can know and understand the vision, the better! For years at Mountain Lake, we offered an event called Newcomer's Lunch where we served lunch, offered childcare, and walked through what our church believed and where we were going. The goal was to get the vision in front of new people quickly, and show them how our vision affected everything we did. We shared stories and showed videos of how the vision worked in real life—how it had changed real lives—and we explained what we were all about. Dozens of new people were inspired each month to become part of the vision.

Vision events always serve as a filter. Not everything makes it through a filter. The same things should be said of our organizations. Not everyone should make it through. Not everyone should stay. The sooner we can explain what we're all about, the sooner we will filter some folks out who have different ideas about what the organization ought to be. If they don't embrace our vision, we send them with blessings on their way to another place. We only want people sticking around who are excited about aligning with our mission. I've always wondered why people leave one church or organization because they don't like it there, and then come to another and try to make that one more like the one they left! Have you ever noticed this? The sooner we can clearly let people know that our vision is not up for sale or debate, the more effectively we filter out people on the front end. The best time to get a divorce is before you get married!

CIRCLE THE WAGONS

As families in the United States began to settle in the West, they would often find themselves in uncharted territory and camped in scary, unfamiliar places. When they set up camp at night, they would have everyone circle up their wagons, and they slept inside that circle. This allowed them to keep an eye on each other, protect each other, and stay alive! The same thing is needed in our organizations. Being mean about the vision requires strategically and consistently circling the wagons with our leaders.

Try looking up all the times Jesus tried to get away from the crowds of people who followed Him.[1] He wasn't *just* trying to get away from people. He wanted to be with His leaders—the disciples. Jesus recognized that in the long run, if His leaders didn't get the vision, none of His followers would. Jesus was the quintessential leader. He understood that influence multiplies more rapidly when the leaders fully understand and embrace the vision.

Retreats, conferences, weekly and monthly meetings, team-building events, volunteer rallies, and other special events are all expressions of circling the wagons. Every time one of these events concluded at Mountain Lake, I would have a leader come up to me and say: "Shawn, thanks for tonight. Honestly I've been struggling lately as a leader and had even thought about quitting; but after tonight I'm re-energized and ready to go!"

Jesus circled with His leaders virtually every day and every night for three years. Think about that. You decide how much less you need to do it than that. Some leadership groups call for weekly circling. Some teams require it monthly, quarterly, or semiannually. However often you decide to meet with your leaders, know this: as the leaders go, so goes the organization.

The more leaders I talk to, the more I realize most don't really understand the importance of the principle of circling the wagons. From time to time I'll get a call from a pastor, and the call will go something like this: "Shawn, I'm struggling with my _____ (position on their staff). They just don't seem to get it. They don't seem to be on board with the vision. We are just not on the same page. Can you help?"

> However often you decide to meet with your leaders, know this: as the leaders go, so goes the organization.

The first thing I usually ask that pastor is, "Well, tell me about your weekly meeting with them."

The answer is usually predictable: "Well, we don't really have a set meeting time right now. We talk all the time, on the phone and via text, but with all the counseling I'm doing and so forth, we haven't really had time for a regular sit-down meeting. I call them or they call me if there's a problem (which there always seems to be)."

Do you see the problem?

Vision alignment among leaders requires two fundamental things: proximity and consistency. We must be with them consistently, or distance decay will prevail. Vision drift will happen. The leak will become too big to plug. I have always told my direct reports that nothing is more important than our regular meeting with each other—nothing! At Mountain Lake, I met one-on-one with my direct reports every week. I met every other week with all our pastors. I met at least once a month with all our staff. I met at least every other month with our finance team and advisory team. All our pastors met monthly with their own leaders. As a church, we met semi-annually with *every* leader in our multicampus church. Now do you see why we had such great vision alignment and buy-in? Being mean about the vision requires circling the wagons consistently.

I know that some leaders reading this are thinking *How does he have time for all of this?* I didn't! I just made time. Keeping the vision in front of my leaders and keeping the vision from leaking in my leaders is the most important part of my leadership of others! I refuse to let anything get in the way of that. These types of meetings go on my calendar first and foremost, and nothing gets in the way of them. There are actually lots of things I don't get to and I'm not as diligent about. Circling up with my leaders cannot be one of those things. To be successful in the vision, you will have to make that choice as well. The vision will dictate your day or the day will dictate your vision.

> Vision alignment among leaders requires two fundamental things: proximity and consistency.

TEACH ON VISION

As I mentioned earlier, most organizations I know have an annual vision day or even an entire month each year dedicated to this idea. Most organizations have special times when they focus on rallying everyone around the mission. But remember—vision leaks. That saltwater lake runs dry. A single day or a month will not do the job of replenishing it. We have got to communicate the vision consistently in creative ways. What could this look like for you?

During my teaching ministry, our entire teaching calendar always formed around the vision. Every teaching series we did was focused on either helping people have a healthy relationship with God or with others, or helping people *Belong, Become,* or *Bless.* Either that's our mission, or it's not! We sought to balance the three in our teaching each year. Belonging focused on the *heart*; becoming focused on the *head* and the *hands*; and blessing focused on the *feet*. Frankly, if it didn't help move people toward God's mission for their lives and our church, we didn't talk about it. We wanted to be consistently clear about our mission and keep everyone in our church focused on it. That's the leader's job!

Do people ever get tired of hearing about a mission so often? Maybe. But at least they know it; and if they know it, more and more of them will love it and share it.

CELEBRATE IT CONSTANTLY

When people serve or work in our organizations, they are often privately wrestling with questions such as, "Does this really matter? Do I matter? Is this really making a difference?" When people give to an organization, they want to know two things: "What happens when I give?" and "What happened because I gave?"

What gets celebrated gets done, because what we celebrate communicates what we value. It highlights the importance of what we're doing. It demonstrates that we're winning. Being mean about the vision requires celebrating every time we see the vision happening in and around our organization.

 What we celebrate communicates what we value.

One of the major mistakes I see leaders make is failing to celebrate privately and publicly when the vision is happening. In John Ortberg's *The Life You've Always Wanted*, he talks about slowing down long enough to truly enjoy God and what He is doing in and around our lives. He calls it the spiritual discipline of celebration.[2] The words *discipline* and *celebration* may not seem to go together, but for me they do. I can totally relate to what Ortberg writes, because for me, celebration is indeed a discipline. I don't celebrate easily. I am a recovering perfectionist. I have a tendency to only see what still needs to be fixed, versus what has been fixed already. Anyone else?

I am naturally a glass-half-empty person. Even when a goal is accomplished, I tend to just move to the next one. I am focused. I am driven. However, the older and more mature I grow as a leader, the more I understand the necessity of celebration, not only for me but for everyone around me. We all need to know that we matter. We all need to know that we're making a difference, and to be reminded that the vision is happening!

Is celebration a discipline for you? Do you know how to enjoy the journey? Are you personally taking time to reflect and celebrate what's happening now in and around you? Think about it and create a plan. Look for ways to celebrate the vision. Circle back around and talk about goals that have been accomplished. Talk about the lives that are being changed. Be specific. Share stories. Ask for testimonies. Give rounds of applause, and display people's accomplishments. Celebrating when the vision actually happens in and through a person's life is the ultimate "atta boy." It cheers people on and moves them to want to be a part of what's happening.

KEEP IT FRESH

I'm making lots of confessions in this book, so while I'm at it, I'll make another one. I'm a vegan. No meat. No dairy. I largely live on a whole-food, plant-based diet. I eat tons of fruits and veggies every week. Yes, I feel great and I have more energy. Don't knock it until you try it! But that's not my point. The toughest transition in becoming a vegan was not abstaining from meat. That was surprisingly easy. The toughest thing was realizing that fresh, whole foods don't last forever in the pantry like packaged, heavily processed foods. You have to keep them fresh. You've also got to be creative. Kale, tofu, and quinoa are now staples in my diet. I had better be creative. Pray for me there.

Being mean about the vision is like being vegan. You have to keep things fresh and creative. When the same fresh food stays out on the counter for too long, what began as something beautiful soon begins to tarnish and even rot. Vision works the same way! The longer the vision is out on the counter (or on the platform or in the boardroom), the more it tends to lose its freshness over time.

Our task as leaders is not only to talk about the vision but also to talk about it in fresh and creative ways. At our church we have often used creative language and metaphors to engage and inspire people toward our collective vision. We like using pop-culture references to get our point across. Whether it's visuals, movie clips, video, drama, games, or stories, they all communicate the vision in fresh ways.

Sometimes keeping things fresh is as simple as paying attention to your tone of voice. Do you remember Charlie Brown's teacher? The incessant, never-ending, boring "Wah, wah, wah, wah, wah," was all anyone ever heard from her. We can't keep things lively with dull, monotonous speaking voices. It doesn't matter how right we are. People are more often persuaded by passion than logic. Being passionate is more important than being articulate. As we present the vision, we need to evoke the emotion that came with it. If the vision doesn't move us, it won't move others. But if it has moved us, it should move others!

We need to let go a little, and speak from one human being to another. Our tone of voice should change. The decibel level needs to go up, and then down. At some point in the talk, we move away from the notes. Genuinely share our hearts. At that point, we step away from the lectern. Our posture is affected. We might stand up or sit down. We're up on our toes or on the edge of our seats. Are we performing or manipulating people? No. This comes from deep inside. We believe God has spoken to us! Is that awesome, or what? The way we communicate should demonstrate that.

> **People are more often persuaded by passion than logic.**

What our listeners need from us is a white-hot passion for the vision. Many times in church staff meetings, I have sat up on the edge of my seat and said something like this:

> Guys, I know this is a difficult decision. I know the task ahead of us is great. But just so you know, I'm not interested in just riding out this comfortable ministry to the end of my career. I'm not interested in just feeding the Megachurch Ministry Machine and keeping it going until I retire. God has given this church a mission. That mission is clear and direct. The mission dictates that we cannot retreat. We cannot stand still. Eternal destinies hang in the balance. Families and communities around the world hang in the balance. What we're doing is the most important

thing in the world. That's why we're taking new ground. That's why I'm on a mission. This church is on a mission. This mission is our calling; so yes, I'm asking you to sacrifice with me and see this thing through.

After I have finished with a conversation like that, I have often looked up to notice that other people are sitting on the edges of their seats too. A few people are fighting back tears. There's a new energy in the room. I give them a moment to respond. I want to hear from them. Do they get it? Are they on board? Are the ready to take the next hill? I want to know if they get the vision. It turns out very often that they do. They just needed to be reminded. The vision becomes fresh again, and we take the next hill together.

Can I challenge you? When was the last time you showed you had some passion about the vision? When was the last time you got emotional about it? When was the last time your voice trembled while you spoke about it? When was the last time you fought back tears as you talked about it in the most genuine way? *Are* you passionate about the vision? Does everyone know it? I'm not asking you to put on a performance, or whip up some tears and pull people's heartstrings for cheap effect. I am asking you to get back to the source. Maybe you need to sit down, reconnect, and plan a way to share it with your people. Maybe you need to throw away the notes and the agenda this week and just share from your heart. Take everyone back to the beginning. Tell the story. Tell everyone why *you* are here. Remind them why this is important and ask them to sacrifice with you. Remember: where there is no vision the people perish. The flip side is also true. Where there *is* a vision, there is life.

In My Journal

▶ Is the vision in danger of becoming stale in our organization? How can I keep it fresh?

▶ Does everyone in our organization know what we value?

▶ How are we holding each other accountable to what we value?

▶ How can we circle the wagons more in our organization to re-cast the vision?

▶ In what ways can we communicate the vision more creatively? Both verbally and visually?

SEVEN

IDENTIFYING A VISION HIJACKER

First, the bad news: no matter how clearly, consistently, or creatively we communicate the vision, some people just won't get it. Sometimes they will not want to follow. Sometimes they will wander. They will have their own ideas—their own agendas. Sometimes they'll even try to hijack the vision!

I don't know how you were raised, but I was told never to pick up hitchhikers. That may sound mean, because after all, hitchhikers obviously need a ride. Why not stop to pick them up? Simply because, historically, hitchhikers have often become hijackers. They've knocked the driver in the head and seized the wheel of the car, and taken both car and driver somewhere against their will. The word *hijack* means "to seize by force or threat of force."[1]

Hijacking happens in organizations every day. The leader gets knocked out of the driver's seat, and the vehicle is taken somewhere else against the leader's will. Here's how it happens: If you think about it, every organization begins 100 percent unified around the vision. It begins completely aligned. Sure, there may be only one person, or just a few people, but everyone believes in the vision so deeply they're willing to risk everything to see it happen. However, over time, new people begin to come on board, many of whom don't understand what the organization really stands for and where it is trying to go. They certainly have different ideas about where it *should* go. Slowly, either consciously or unconsciously, vision hitchhikers often become vision hijackers. If we don't wake up and seize the wheel, we're going to end up miles away from our original destination. Our first task is learning to recognize potential vision hijackers. What do they look like?

> Slowly, either consciously or unconsciously, vision hitchhikers often become vision hijackers.

UNINTENTIONAL HIJACKERS

Sometimes hitchhikers don't even realize it when they slip their hands onto the wheel. They are what I call unintentional vision hijackers. They're not trying to take control of the mission—or at least they don't realize they are. They actually have the best of intentions. They just like to drive. They like to be in control. Whether they realize it or not, they begin to reveal through their words and actions that they have different ideas about the direction everyone should go.

Unintentional vision hijackers will often say they are totally on board with the vision, but then they'll consistently make comments like: "Well, at my last church . . ." or "At my last job . . ." or "In my experience . . ." Comments like these are usually made by folks who don't yet understand what we're trying to do, and they're still operating on a paradigm they're familiar with from their past.

Again, most of the time, these people don't intend any harm. They're not intentionally trying to take the steering wheel of the organization. They just don't understand where we're headed yet. They don't know of any other destination than the ones they've already been to, and they will unconsciously try to steer things back in that old direction. They're so blinded by their past experiences that they just can't visualize a new destination, and it makes them nervous. They probably aren't maliciously trying to bring down the organization. They just don't know any better. They're nervous. They're scared. And we can help them. We can show them the way and get them there if they're willing to make the trip.

Years ago, an executive pastor at a large church told me about a conversation he had with an elderly disgruntled church member in a deli. After picking up his sandwich at the counter, he was on his way back to his table, when a man stopped him.

"Can I ask you a question?" the man asked.

"Sure," the pastor responded.

"Why are you all constantly making such a big deal about joining a small group at your church? I just don't understand. In my last church [see it coming?] we did Sunday school at the building and it seemed to work great. I don't understand this whole 'small groups in homes' phenomenon. At my last church, I had close friends in my Sunday-school class. We miss Sunday school here and I don't see why we can't have that option."

Now first of all, for years when someone would question our church's philosophy or vision, I would become literally "mean" more rapidly. Not a good approach. However, when this pastor friend of mine told me about his response to this man's question, it changed how I responded to unintentional vision hijackers. Here's what the pastor told me:

"Shawn, I immediately realized that this man's concerns were raised out of his own lack of understanding. His questions were largely based on the fact that he understood only one way of doing things. I recognized this encounter with this man as an opportunity. So I told him, 'I'd love to answer your question. Can I pull up a chair?'"

For the next ten minutes, this pastor spelled out in detail why he was so passionate about small groups meeting in homes. He began by saying that he believed they offered a better discipling environment for most people. He explained that small groups in homes reflected the New Testament paradigm of discipleship more accurately than Sunday school. He went on to explain the church's desire to cultivate transparence, authenticity, and intimacy, and why he believed that small groups in homes provided the best environment for these. He spoke about the New Testament model of pastoral care, and explained that small groups were much more than a class or a Bible study, but a group of people to do life with seven days a week. He explained there was no way a pastor of a church could know about all of the needs of a hundred people, much less five thousand—and then truly know and care for them all. Small groups allowed the church family to help take care of the church family. You get the point.

After the pastor had rattled on for a while, he paused and said, "As you can see, I'm passionate about this. Sorry. But does any of this make sense?" The man responded: "Yes it does, and honestly, I've never thought about it like you just explained it. It sounds like a no-brainer for us. It sounds like we need to join a small group." Mission accomplished!

My goal here is not to get into a debate about whether Sunday school or small groups are a more effective means of discipleship. My point in sharing all this is simply to point out the fact that many people become unintentional vision hijackers solely because they don't know any other way of doing things than the way they've done them in the past. They need to be "discipled" in *why* we do what we do.

These situations and people present opportunities to slow down long enough to explain to them that all-important *why*. When we take the time to paint a clear picture of where we're going and why it's best for our organizations that we go there, we can shepherd people effectively in one direction. Sometimes vision hijackers can morph back into vision hitchhikers. They get it. They embrace the vision, and come along with us for the ride. Then again, some don't.

VISION MAVERICKS

Some hitchhikers are just up to no good. They are going the direction they are going because they like calling their own shots. They drift from one place to another, looking to stir up some action and adventure. Some hitchhikers have a rebellious streak. They get used to their own way of doing things. They are lone rangers. They are what I call vision mavericks.

The scariest thing to me about vision mavericks is the fact that they tend to be some of the most gifted people you've ever met. They're intelligent. They're extroverted. People love talking to them. Vision mavericks stand out from the rest of the crowd. They usually have highly charismatic personalities. They are natural leaders. When they join an organization, they build friendships quickly. They build circles of influence. When they speak, people tend to listen. Mavericks have usually been leaders or have led people and initiatives in the past. They may have even been successful in the past in some sort of leadership, and often in a high-level career. They can tell a good story. They can make a good first impression. They can be convincing. We tend to be impressed by vision mavericks.

At first, vision mavericks don't seem like mavericks at all. They make us laugh. They're good with people. They tell us they love us. They tell us they love it in our organization—that they love where we are going. They say they are glad to be along for the ride, and they are on board with where we're headed. But the longer we listen to and observe them, the more we grow concerned. The longer they are around, the more we recognize we might not all be reading from the same page of the playbook.

Vision mavericks have lots of ideas and suggestions. Some of them are good ideas, and well . . . you know what I mean. Remember that there's a difference between a good idea and a God idea. Some ideas serve the vision, and some don't. Vision mavericks often have ideas that have agenda attached to them, but that is hard to spot at first. This is one of the reasons we should be slower to place people into leadership positions in our organizations. Mavericks want to lead. They want a platform. They want to teach something—as soon as possible.

1 Timothy 3 cautions church leaders about putting people into leadership too quickly, without knowing their true character and reputation. We can filter out some vision mavericks by slowing down our leadership placement process. For years at Mountain Lake Church where I served, before anyone could lead a small group Bible Study, they had to have been in a group as a participant for at least six months. Most of the time, it was for a year or more. We rarely placed someone into an influential role without allowing some time to pass to test someone's character. Vision mavericks usually want to lead but cannot follow. The kinds of leaders we are looking for must know how to do both.

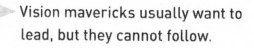 Vision mavericks usually want to lead, but they cannot follow.

Vision mavericks have strong opinions about the way things ought to be done. And because they tend to be strong personalities themselves, they tend to be very vocal. When they're vocal in encouragement, we appreciate it. But they can also be very vocal in their criticisms—to others. They often have a beef with something the leader is doing. They would do it differently. Vision mavericks don't have a problem leading. They have a problem following.

Honestly, in all my years of ministry, I have never had anyone walk up to me and say: "Shawn, I am against the vision of this church." On the contrary. I have had hundreds say to me: "Shawn, I totally believe in the vision of this church. It's just that I'm struggling with [insert complaint]." First of all, we all need to understand this about vision: Everything we do flows out of the vision. Values are part of the vision. Programming, budgets, curriculum, culture, even the music in our church are part of the vision. Teaching is part of the vision. The children's ministry, student ministry, small-group ministry—it all comes back to the same thing. If someone continues struggling with how we approach any of these things, they are struggling with the vision.

For years I had people walk up to me and say: "Shawn, my family is 100 percent behind the vision. We just struggle with the church's small-group philosophy." I always responded by saying that our small-group philosophy is one of the core components of our vision. If they struggle with our small-group philosophy, they are struggling with the vision! Remember what being mean about the vision is all about. It's about being intentional. If we are intentional about *why* we're doing *what* we're doing, then everything we do is part of the vision.

I don't mean, by the way, that people in our organizations can't push to make things better. I don't mean that people can't have ideas and suggestions. I don't mean that people can't challenge the process from time to time. As leaders we need to be willing to listen to people's feedback and suggestions. So how and when is listening to feedback and suggestions appropriate? First, consider the source. I will listen to feedback and constructive critiques from one, and only one, category of person: the kind who loves God, loves the vision, and loves me. If I'm convinced of that, then I can trust that their feedback most likely is free from ulterior motives, and is welcome in my life and organization. I'm open to a critique any day by someone I know loves God and loves me.

Vision mavericks are different. Vision mavericks seem to care more about their preferences than they do about people. They seem to have an agenda. They are struggling because they have a hard time following. When there is a true vision maverick looming and we don't deal with it, it's going to bite us. It has bitten me . . . and I have lived to tell the story.

MAVERICK REDEMPTION

Is there any hope for vision mavericks? Yes, there is. In the right set of circumstances, a vision maverick can be redeemed. Years ago when Mountain Lake was a fledgling church that had just started meeting in a cafeteria for weekly worship services, we experienced a great vision test. We had about a hundred people coming every week. One of the bright spots in our ministry was a guy by the name of, let's just say "Don" (not his real name). Don was gifted. He was smart. He was knowledgeable about the Bible and experienced in church leadership. Don quickly became a leader in our church.

Don was a very caring, compassionate person and a good Bible counselor and teacher. He grew in influence in our church. He was a servant. He was my friend. However, a few months into his church membership, I began to get these e-mails from him every once in a while. In these e-mails, which would sometimes be quite long, Don would tell me about how things were going in his small group, and then begin to offer a few "suggestions." Many of his suggestions he claimed, came out of struggles people in his group were having with our church. He would admit he struggled with some of these things as well.

Several times, on the heels of one of these long e-mails, I would schedule a meeting with Don. I wanted to make sure that we were all on the same page. He would always assure me that we were. He would always tell me he felt better and things made more sense after we talked. He assured me he would sort out things with people in his group. It would go quiet again. Things would seem to get better. All seemed well. Six or eight weeks would go by and then I would get another e-mail from Don. He was struggling again, and his group was struggling with some of what we were doing.

Could we have a large group of people struggling with the vision of the church? I thought. One by one I began to question a few members of Don's group. It turned out most of them had no major beefs with the church. Sure they had a question here and there, but nothing major. A few of them told me that any concerns they had actually arose out of some things Don had said in their group. Several of them told me Don had often voiced concerns about the church's way of doing things.

I slowly began to recognize there was a common denominator in all of this: Don. It turns out not everyone who says they are behind the vision is actually behind the vision. People can be hiding behind their own agendas, ambitions, opinions, and preferences.

Because they are often hiding, vision mavericks are often hard to locate or recognize. They might be on the front lines of leadership, and yet they're secretly sabotaging everything we're trying to do!

> It turns out not everyone who says they are behind the vision is actually behind the vision.

When Jesus sent His disciples out to carry on the mission He had started, He told them to be "as wise as serpents and harmless as doves" (Matt. 10:16 KJV). Jesus was telling them that when they went out to heal and teach people, because of the power and the following they had, people would try to take advantage of them. Jesus told them to first be harmless as doves. Have pure motives. Be gentle. Believe the best of people. Be harmless. However, on the flip side, Jesus told them to be as wise as serpents. This word *wise* can mean "shrewd" or "crafty." It's akin to the word used to describe the serpent that tricked Eve in Genesis chapter 3: "Now the serpent was more crafty [shrewd] than any of the wild animals the LORD God had made" (v. 1). Jesus told His leaders to be as wise as serpents. Be discerning. Be shrewd. Be on your guard. Believe in people, but don't let people take advantage of you—or the vision. Don't allow people to bully you! Be strong. Be mean about the vision!

I learned this the hard way with Don. One day after another long, passive-aggressive e-mail from Don, I called him and told him we needed to meet again. I told him I loved him, but it was becoming obvious to me that he and our church were not on the same page regarding the vision and direction of our small-group philosophy, and therefore the philosophy of our church. I told him that until we sorted out his struggles, I thought it best he take a break from leading the small group that met in his home. At this time Don had about twenty-five adults coming to his home each week. I could tell in the meeting that Don was becoming increasingly agitated, but I reiterated that I loved him and I believed in him as a leader. I told him that I wanted to be his pastor. However, if this was going to be the case in the future, he was going to need to demonstrate his willingness to be completely behind the vision of our church before he could be a leader again.

How did Don respond? His first response was, "Shawn, you can't tell me that I can't have a Bible study in my house." He was defiant. He was determined. He was entrenched as a leader who had a platform, and he was not going to let go of that influence. I knew this was going to cause some fallout.

What Don didn't count on, however, was my resolve. I again clearly articulated my call for him to step down as a small group leader, and I let him know we would be following up with every person in his group to let them know this action had been requested by our church, due to a difference in direction and vision. I asked Don once again to please honor the call that I had made. He told me he would "pray about it." As you might imagine, Don and his family left the church after that conversation. On the way out, he took lots of jabs and did lots of damage.

As we made phone calls to the members of Don's group, some were glad we called, some were hurt, and some were defiant. They loved Don. He had played a pivotal role in their spiritual journeys. They had become close friends with Don. Their kids had become close with his kids. Many of them admitted to struggling with the decision I had made, but said they understood. Some told me they didn't understand. To make a long story short, over the next few weeks and months, more than twenty-five adults and their families left our church. These families represented a fourth of our church attendance. Many of them were tithers! Many of them had been hurt by all of this, and they took some jabs on the way out as well.

The first negative cloud had settled over our church. In the subsequent weeks there were other conversations where this drama boiled to the top again and again. Multiple relationships had been affected. People didn't understand. People had been hurt. And hurt people hurt people.

I learned firsthand though this experience that one bad apple really can spoil the whole bunch. The apostle Paul said it this way:

> You were running a good race. Who cut in on you to keep you from obeying the truth? That kind of persuasion does not come from the one who calls you. "*A little yeast works through the whole batch of dough.*" (Gal. 5:7–9, emphasis added)

I learned with Don that indeed, "a little yeast works through the whole batch of dough." The longer we allow disunity to go unaddressed, the more it will fester, spread, and grow. Our church eventually recovered. It took a year or more to heal completely, but we did, and we moved on. Churches usually do, but this kind of thing can leave a scar for a season. But we were committed to see the vision through. We moved forward as a church.

But that's not the end of the story. Fast-forward ten years. Our church had now grown to more than two thousand people and had been through three different building projects. One Sunday, as we finished up a large Newcomer's Lunch event, I looked up and guess who I saw? Don. I didn't know it, but he had been coming back to our church for several weeks. After the lunch was over, Don made a beeline for me. I had no idea what was about to happen. But as Don approached me, and my eyes met his, I saw huge tears begin to well up in his eyes. When he finally got to me, he fell on my shoulder and began to weep.

"I'm sorry," he said. "I'm so sorry. Could you ever forgive me?" Don went on to say, "Shawn, I have had a rebellious spirit for years now. It has now cost me my job, my relationship with my wife, and my children. I realize now it also cost me the best church I have ever been a part of. I have repented to God for my rebellious spirit and if you could ever forgive me and take me back into this church, I will be your biggest fan, and support this church 100 percent."

The whole experience was amazing. Don experienced a lot of healing that day. I think I did, as well. Of course, I forgave him. Our church didn't allow him to be placed into leadership overnight. He actually had to wait for nearly three years for that (remember, harmless as a dove, wise as a serpent). Today, however, Don serves as a valuable leader at Mountain Lake Church! Over the years, through several experiences like this, I have learned to identify potential vision hijackers more readily. I am also reminded to never lose hope—or resolve. The vision must be protected at all costs. I'll continue to show you how in the next chapter.

In My Journal

▸ How can I discern the difference between a critique and a criticism in my organization?

▸ How can I be more discerning in identifying potential vision hijackers?

▸ What might the potential fallout look like when a vision hijacker is not dealt with?

▸ How can I deal with potential hijackers, while displaying care and compassion?

EIGHT

KEEPING THE VISION FROM BEING HIJACKED

One of the main goals of this book is to save you some of the pain I've experienced. So what are the choices we can make now to save us pain and vision drift later? How can we proactively keep the vision from being hijacked?

BE CAREFUL WITH NEW LEADERS

First of all, as I learned with my friend Don, we need to be very careful about who we allow into leadership in our organizations. Leadership is a privilege, not a right. Tenure does not guarantee leadership, but it does make it a safer bet. The old adage "hire slow and fire fast" applies most to leaders. We need to be slow in placing people into positions of power.

Over the years we learned that when we hired a new pastor, we should be slower in giving them a platform until we knew for sure they were a good fit with the team and the vision. I have too often made the mistake of platforming a new leader too quickly and selling that person as the latest Superman or Superwoman who would take our organization to the new level, only to realize within the first year that this person wasn't going to be a good fit on our team.

For years, I got down on myself when leaders would leave our team within the first two years. Then I ran across some research that Jim Collins had done for his book *Built to Last* (look back at chapter 3 for a more detailed discussion). You'll remember that even though you'd think there would be a big difference in the turnover ratios between good companies and great companies, great companies actually had just as much turnover, but usually only within the first eighteen months or so. Great companies tend to have completely unique cultures, as opposed to the rest of corporate America where toxic behavior is often tolerated. Because of that, people usually figure out in a hurry whether they can make the adjustment to the new culture or not. So people usually either exit within the first eighteen months, or they tend to be with the organization for a long time.[1]

I have a friend who recently joined the team of the Lampo Group, led by Dave Ramsey. When he joined the team, he was introduced to what Dave calls "the Nebraska years." These are the years early on in Dave's organization, when Dave first sends leaders to speak to dozens of people (not hundreds) in less populated areas (like Nebraska). Dave wants to give them smaller platforms first, while they're all deciding if this is going to work out in the long run.

The Nebraska years also allow a leader to grow into the job and develop without being thrown into the deep end of the pool too quickly. Dave has learned a critical truth firsthand: don't platform new leaders too quickly.

 Don't platform new leaders too quickly.

There is no foolproof way to know whether a leader will fit before they are on the team. However, there are many steps we can take to increase our odds of selecting leaders who can and will fit into our organizational culture. Over the years, as I selected new team members, I sought to evaluate them by four equally critical components. Most of us have heard of some variation of the Four C's: *Character, Capacity, Chemistry,* and *Calling.* This is not a book on hiring, so I won't bore you with those details now. But two of these aspects in particular are the most overlooked on the front end.

Don't Overlook Character

So many leaders spend so much time assessing a candidate's capacity that they often overlook the critical component of character. Why is a new candidate leaving their old job? Is everyone else at fault where they work now? Is everyone else wrong? Are they running toward something or away from something? Are they well thought of by their peers? What kind of relationship do they have with their current supervisor? Do they have a good reputation? Do they live a life the Bible describes as being "above reproach" (1 Tim. 3:2)? This phrase means "blameless" or "without accusation."

To find this out, we not only call references, but we get permission to call references of references. We ask the candidate to give us the name of a person who doesn't like them very much right now. What would this person say about them? We want to know how this person responds to authority. We want to know how this person responds when they're told no. Do they have a good relationship with their parents? How about their spouse, if they're married? On a scale of one to ten, how would their spouse rate their marriage? (Yep, we're not afraid to get personal.)

We listen carefully in our interviews. If the candidate will run down their boss now, they probably will later. If they have had a lot of conflict where they are now, they probably will later. If everyone else is wrong in their organization now, they probably will think everyone else is wrong here too. All these things are used to help determine their character. If they lack character, odds are they will never support a vision other than their own.

Don't Overlook Chemistry

People believe in us before they believe in the vision. That's why leaders in an organization have to *like* each other. There has to be relational chemistry. We have to like each other to trust each other. We have to trust each other to share the same vision. And inevitably, we are going to be put in positions where we're going to need to have each other's backs. Chemistry is incredibly important. I believe our top-tier leaders also need to be our friends. As the senior leader, you may be their boss, but you had also better be their friend. You will need them to be your friend in return. They will take arrows for you, so they had better like and trust you. Relational chemistry makes all of this possible.

We don't have to be best friends and go on vacation together. We don't have to hang out away from the office all that often. We do need to know each other. We do need to love each other. We do need to like each other.

How do we assess relational chemistry? Spend extended time with people. Spend several days working together. Play eighteen rounds of golf with them. Attend a sporting event together. Go fishing together. Perhaps an overnight retreat with the executive team is in order. The higher the level of leadership, the more time you should spend with them before hiring them.

Confront Things and People Quickly

How do we know when to confront vision drift? Years ago, I heard my friend Mark Beeson, pastor of Granger Community Church, in Granger, Indiana, say: "The most dangerous deviations from the vision are those situations where someone is just 1 percent off. Its easier to spot and deal with someone who's diametrically opposed to the vision than it is with someone who's just barely off." You tell me: What happens when two objects are traveling the same direction at the same velocity but is just one degree off, in terms of trajectory? You guessed it: they get farther apart over time. Eventually they can end up miles away from each other.

This proves that the sooner we confront any perceived vision drift the better. It's going to be better for us, better for the drifting person, and better for the organization. We don't need to wait until we're positive that there's a problem to confront it. We need to nip it in the bud. Approaching each situation with a spirit of humility, as I outlined earlier, allows us to confront any potential vision drift early, without accusing someone.

Once we have leaders on board, there are always going to be vision leaks with team members. Remember: I have learned the hard way that a little yeast does indeed work itself through the whole batch of dough. This means we must deal quickly with potential problems, as with the situation I described with Don in the last chapter. As leaders, we can never just stick our heads in the sand and hope vision issues will go away. They almost never do, without great harm. We can't be cowards. We can't be intimidated by big personalities, big givers, people with lots of influence, or long-tenured employees, citizens, or church members. We must confront vision drift quickly!

The great challenge with this, of course, is the fact that most of us hate confrontation. Don't you? I still hate it. I never want to do it. I want to pretend the issue will go away. I want to delegate it to someone else. But I can't. As the leader, my primary job, of course, is to protect the vision! If the vision gets hijacked on my watch, I am responsible for that. Confrontation is critical in protecting the vision. Most of us tend to think confrontation is a negative thing, but the Bible actually encourages us to confront each other:

> If another believer sins against you, go privately and point out the offense. If the other person listens and confesses it, you have won that person back. But if you are unsuccessful, take one or two others with you and go back again, so that everything you say may be confirmed by two or three witnesses. If the person still refuses to listen, take your case to the church. If he or she won't accept the

church's decision, treat that person as a pagan or a corrupt tax collector. (Matt. 18:15–17 NLT)

Therefore, if you are offering your gift at the altar and there remember that your brother or sister has something against you, leave your gift there in front of the altar. First go and be reconciled to them; then come and offer your gift. (Matt. 5:23–24)

In other words, the Bible says that when we have an issue with someone, we are to go to that person and confront the issue. When we realize someone has an issue with us, we are to go and confront the issue. We are never to wait for someone else to come to us. We make the first move. If we don't confront people about issues, we're being disobedient to God. We're cowards. It's that simple.

No one is exempt from the need of confrontation. If this is true for people in general, how much more should it be true for leaders? We should be the ones modeling the way in our organizations. We set the culture—and since culture is more caught than taught, we need to show how to approach these situations in a healthy, redemptive manner. The longer we wait, the rougher it's going to get, and the greater the potential damage. We have the power to save everyone that pain.

Remember that when we started this journey, I said being mean about the vision doesn't give us a license to be mean to people. Confrontation doesn't give us a license to be critical. Some people enjoy confrontation. I think if you enjoy confrontation, you need counseling! When we confront, it should always scare us into sensitivity. When we confront, it should be out of love for God and people and love for the vision God has given us. When we confront, it should be gentle, respectful, and helpful. We should always seek to be redemptive. "Brothers, if anyone is caught in any transgression, you who are spiritual should restore him in a spirit of gentleness" (Gal. 6:1 ESV).

What does this look like in real life? I have role-played through the following scenario with our pastors dozens of times over the years, to help equip them with the art of confrontation. The role-play is based in fact. I have lived out this situation countless times over my decades in vocational ministry. When I realize that there is a transgression against the vision or against me, or I get a sense that someone is struggling with me or with the vision, I will call them up and say:

Hey! I would love to buy you lunch or coffee sometime soon and catch up. I also have something I wanted to talk to you about. I would love to get together this week if you have time.

I won't take no for an answer, by the way. Then once we get to that meeting I will say something like:

I have so enjoyed you being a part of the ministry here. I love you and your family so much. God has used you in some remarkable ways around here. I'm thankful for you and I care about you. That's precisely why I wanted to talk to you because lately it just seems like something's not right. It could be totally me. It could be something I ate. I may be reading too much into things, but I have just sensed that you might be struggling with things here at the church, or even struggling with me.

I will often go on to point out a specific situation that has led me to think this way:

It could be me, but the other day in the lobby (or in the staff meeting), your body language and tone just seemed to communicate there might be something going on between you and me or between you and the ministry.

Sometimes I will say:

The other day when you said _____ [insert passive-aggressive jab], I just read between the lines and began to think there might be something deeper going on here.

I'll finish by saying:

Again, it could be totally me, but that's just the vibe I got. Does any of this makes sense to you?

Then I listen. It *could* be totally me, by the way. I could be wrong. They could have had a tough time recently. I might be a little insecure in some way about the state of our relationship. On the other hand, they might have deep struggles with me that neither of us is fully aware of. My hope is to invite this person's struggles, if any, out into the open. I want to give them a safe place to be honest.

I have not accused. I have not brought up hearsay. I have let them know my assumptions could even be wrong.

"No! There's nothing wrong! I'm great! Everything is great!" is often the response. It would be wonderful if that were always true. But sometimes the person will deny that they're struggling with the vision, even if they are. I usually won't argue with them in the first conversation. I'll take them at their word; and at the very worst, potential hijackers know I've got my eye on them and their passive-aggressive behavior won't be tolerated.

Provide a Place for Honesty

I have found that about 75 percent of the time, when I provide a safe place for a person to be honest about their struggles with the organization's vision, they will take the opportunity. The person sitting across from me during that conversation will often open up and say: "Well, now that you mention it, there are some things I'm struggling with."

Here we go. Now we are about to get honest. I'm not going to be defensive. I'm going to listen. I'm going to be calm. I'm not going to react. If it turns out their problem is indeed with the vision, I'll wait for them to finish complaining and critiquing. Then I will often say:

Well, _____ [name], I appreciate you being honest with me. This really helps me understand where you're coming from. That helps me as the leader. However, you need to know that the things you're struggling with have everything to do with the vision we believe God has given us. We're not going to change it or veer away from it, and if I'm going to be your pastor, you are going to have to die to yourself and embrace that vision. If you can't then we don't need to work together. If you can, then we should!

I will usually conclude the conversation by saying:

Well, the most important thing for you and me as leaders in our church is that we are on the same page regarding the vision of our church. If we can do this, that's great. I would love to be your pastor and leader. However, if you don't think you can in good conscience be behind the vision, you are going to be miserable, and you are not going to be helping our church. I want to give you a week to think and pray about this and then I want us to get back together and I want to hear from you. That will determine where we go from here.

I have now put the ball in their court. They are making a decision. They will decide the next steps.

GRACE AND TRUTH IN LOVE

How do we approach all these situations? We follow the example of Jesus. The Bible describes the posture in which He came: "For the law was given through Moses; grace and truth came through Jesus Christ" (John 1:17). He was full of grace and compassion. However, He didn't back away from the truth. He always called it as He saw it, even if it upset people. That's what got Him killed! The Bible says we are all to walk as Jesus did. And how did Jesus walk into every conversation? Full of grace and truth.

Being full of grace means we give people the benefit of a doubt. It means we believe the best about people—that we accept people's imperfections and even forgive them of the sins they commit against us or our organizations.

Being full of grace means we approach each situation as a secure leader. There are too many insecure leaders in our world who believe that everyone everywhere is a threat. We need to be secure enough in our own skin to believe that not everybody is out to take us down or take down the vision. Again, I believe that most people don't realize that their words or actions could be undermining the vision. What they need most of the time is just some coaching and teaching, and a revelation of how their words and actions are being interpreted. We can help them see their blind spots and teach them how to support the vision in word and deed. In the church, we call this discipleship.

At the same time, we need not back away from the truth. We need to be honest. Many pastors I know are people pleasers, and too often tell people what they want to hear rather than what they need to hear. We will go home and talk to our spouse about someone, but we won't say it to the person's face. This is gossip. It's dishonest, and I believe we are going to be held accountable by God for that. We must speak the truth. We must be blatantly honest. We can't beat around the bush. We owe every team member, staff member, and church member complete honesty. If we want them to be honest with us, we must be honest with them. That's speaking the truth.

Let's look at one more Scripture verse that speaks to this issue. In Ephesians 4, the apostle Paul is writing about how Christians are to share the message of Jesus with people when he says: "We will speak the truth in love, growing in every way more and more like Christ, who is the head of his body, the church" (v.15 NLT). Two thousand years later, many Christians have done a lot to harm the image of Jesus, the image of the church, and the image of all Christians, by speaking the truth *not* in love. The same thing can happen when it comes to confronting vision drift.

When we approach someone in this situation, our goal should be not just to do the right thing for the organization. We should also seek to do what's best for those involved. We confront vision drift because we love people—because we want them to win. We confront because we want people to be fulfilled in their work. We confront people in the church with their divisive words or actions because we want to help them see their blind spots. We want to help them grow, and to teach them how to resolve conflict. We want to teach them that this kind of "venting" or complaining to another person is not biblical. We want to teach them that nowhere in the Bible does it say, "If you need to get this off your chest, go talk to someone else about it." I've never been able to find that verse. They need to know that. The goal of every confrontation is to redeem relationships and protect the vision we believe God has given us for our lives and our organizations.

> The goal of every confrontation is to redeem relationships and protect the vision.

Confronting in love means we don't accuse. We don't point the finger. We don't cast blame. We don't raise our voice. We are not angry. We take the high road. We give people an opportunity to explain. We believe them when they explain it. We balance grace and truth! Love at the expense of truth is wrong; but truth at the expense of love is also wrong.

HOW CAN WE POSSIBLY DO THIS?

So what can motivate us to lean into the conversations nobody wants to have? It's this: when we confront vision drift, we save lives and organizations. It's as simple as that.

We save lives because we potentially keep people from going down a path of self-destruction. We save organizations because we keep the whole organization from being infected. If we don't confront, this issue will rarely just go away. It will spread. It will damage.

Many of you may be realizing at this moment that you have to take action on this. You may need to take a break from reading this book and go do what a leader is supposed to do: courageously confront vision drift with grace and truth, speaking the truth in love. For God's sake. For the vision's sake. For the other person's sake. For your sake. That decision alone would be worth far more than the price of this book. It could save your organization. It could save the vision. It could save someone's life and relationships. It could save you. Let me know how it goes.[2]

In My Journal

▸ What role does vision play in my discussions with potential leaders?

▸ With whom do I need to have a courageous conversation regarding the vision? Why?

▸ How and when will I do it?

▸ How will I balance grace and truth? Speak the truth in love?

NINE

WHEN IT'S NOT WORKING OUT

So what do we do when things just don't get better? What do we do when we've confronted, we've been clear, we've given honest feedback? What do we do after we've coached and challenged, and been honest with a team member, and nothing changes? That is the subject of this chapter.

I have spent a large part of my life in school. I graduated from high school fourteenth in my class. I have a BS in business administration. I have a master's degree from seminary. The coursework covered a lot of topics. But did you know that in all of my classes, we never once talked about how to respond when things weren't working out with an employee? Not one time did we ever talk about how to release someone—how to fire someone. I wish they had!

No one ever told me how to do it. No one ever helped me prepare for those times when I would hire someone and then realize it wasn't working out as I had hoped. I used to beat myself up in times like these. I would question myself. Sometimes I knew it had been my fault. Sometimes I've lacked a good hiring and selection process that effectively screens candidates. Sometimes I got in too big of a hurry. Some of the worst hires I have made have come over a lunch or dinner table when I said: "Man, I like you! Will you come work for me?" Those kinds of hires usually don't turn out so well. Too many times I have hired too quickly and fired too slowly. I have the scars to prove it.

Here's some good news: no one is perfect. That means no one hires perfectly. No matter how rigorous our hiring process, sometimes it just doesn't turn out well. Sometimes the organization just changes, or the team member changes. Perhaps the team member simply hits a rough patch. Or maybe the employee fools us! When we realize we got it wrong, the truth is, it doesn't matter how it happened. We can live in the past, or we can deal with this issue at hand. We must decide.

When it is wrong, for whatever reason, we need the courage to make it right. Sometimes this will mean coaching. Sometimes this will mean offering counseling or moving them to a different seat on the bus. As a last resort, a team member will need to be released. I am going to talk about this scenario here, because no one ever talked with me about it. I don't want that to be the case with you!

> When it is wrong, for whatever reason, we need the courage to make it right.

WHAT WE OWE OUR TEAM

Before we get into the specifics of when and how to release a staff person, let's review everything we owe our team members before that moment comes.

Grace

We owe every team member grace. We should not expect perfection. We should overlook offenses and flaws, and give team members time to morph, grow, and change. We should never react rashly when an employee makes a mistake. Rather, we owe it to employees to sit down with them later, when cooler heads can prevail, and debrief on the issue. Just because we are the leaders, that doesn't empower us to chew out, yell at, demean, or embarrass team members.

We should forgive. We should love. Team members need to believe that we always have their best interests at heart. They need to know that we are here to help them, and to hear that in the meantime, we don't expect perfection. If grace helps change us, then grace helps change others too.

Honesty

We owe each team member honesty. Years ago I heard Pastor Bill Hybels of Willow Creek Community Church speak about conversations that cover "the last 10 percent." The idea was that in most of our day-to-day interactions, we deal in the safety of exposing 90 percent of ourselves, but we hide the last 10 percent: the stuff that makes for awkward conversations. Hybels explained that when a tough conversation needs to happen we should set a culture where we approach a person and ask permission to have a "last-10-percent conversation" where we are totally honest with each other.

I have always loved that because it's true. We all hold back. We do so out of fear of rocking the boat, feeling awkward in a conversation, and lots of other reasons. Now, we will often share our last 10 percent with someone else if they're in our innermost circle. We will talk to our spouse or best friend about it. But in confrontational situations, we often lack the courage to be completely honest with the other person when we are in the room with them. It's cowardly, if you think about it.

I have always felt like it lacked integrity for me to go home to my spouse and vent about a team member if I had not been completely honest with the person. So I've intentionally made a commitment to every new team member under my supervision, that I would never tell my wife something about them that I am not willing to say to them directly. They would never have to wonder what I really thought. They would never have to wonder if they were doing a great job. They would never have to wonder about the areas where they needed to improve. I was going to say it. I was going to be honest with them.

In my regular meetings with team members, I would often offer words of encouragement based on how they were doing. I would also address specific coaching areas. I would debrief on situations, conversations, and events of the past week or month. My goal was always to help them grow—even help them see their blind spots. I owe them that. If I don't help my team members see their blind spots, who will?

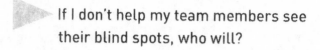 **If I don't help my team members see their blind spots, who will?**

When I sit down with a team member, my goal is not to tell that person what they want to hear. My goal is to help them. That cannot and will not happen without honesty. I am going to call it like I see it. I realize that may sound harsh for some, but on the flip side, how many of us have been lied to by our supervisors? How many of us have felt at times that our bosses weren't being completely honest with us? How many of us have wondered how we're doing because no one ever tells us? See, honesty builds trust, growth, and health among team members. And it builds morale.

If a team member is surprised by being released from our team, I have not done my job effectively. I have not been completely honest. If I'm going to release them, I owe them lots of honest conversations up to that moment, and during that moment. I said earlier that I have fired only three people in all my years of ministry. However, many more have fired themselves. When we are honest with team members, many times they figure out before we do that things might not be working out. God uses those conversations to help people figure out where they fit and where they don't. These conversations help them discover what they are good at and what they are not. Team members will realize when they are knocking it out of the park, but also when the organization is outpacing them.

There have been dozens of times over the years, in the midst of numerous honest conversations, when a team member has come to me and said: "Hey, it's been great here, but I feel like it's time for me to go," or "I've accepted a position at another place." No one else knew it at the time, but they were often firing themselves. Honesty on our part helps team members be honest with themselves about who they are, what they are good at, and where they fit. On the flip side, honesty has helped many more team members grow, develop, morph, and thrive in the long run! Isn't that what we want? Either way, we win, the organization wins, and the team member wins. I had a pastor friend tell me once: "Shawn, our job is always to leave them better off than when we found them." This approach is centered on doing just that.

Clarity and Accountability

Our team members also deserve clarity about the expectations we have for them. What's the only thing worse than a team member not knowing where the target is? A leader who doesn't communicate where the target is. Mapping out distinct goals and setting definitive deadlines gives everyone a clear understanding of what the expectations are. Without clear expectations, team members don't have the chance to experience the thrill of hitting the bull's-eye.

A cohesive vision requires clarity; but it also requires accountability. When a value or aspect of the vision is violated, we must hold each other accountable. We must call each other on the carpet. We must give each other consistent honest feedback as to whether we are all hitting the bull's-eye or not.

In the churches and organizations I have led, our teams conducted six-month reviews, as many organizations do. We called them Performance and Development Reviews. I chose to make "sharing the vision" one of the criteria by which every team member was evaluated. From what I can see, do they believe in the vision? Are they communicating and sharing it with passion with others? Do I feel their excitement for the vision? Why or why not? A team member can be rated unacceptable, acceptable, good, very good, or excellent in this category, just like all the others. When we walk out of those review meetings, we are all clear about the areas where team members are excelling and those areas where they are not.

Proper Placement

We owe our team members a fair shake in the right position that fits their skills and strengths. I have always felt it was my responsibility to help team members recognize and affirm their gifts and strengths, and to coach them through weaknesses and limitations. The wise King Solomon said: "Be sure you know the condition of your flocks; give careful attention to your herds" (Prov. 27:23). We need to be close enough to our team to be able to know the condition of the team—and its members.

I am a big believer in spiritual gifts. We all have them. They are unique to us. They are also unique to our team. God has placed us where we are with a purpose in mind. This also means that none of us is gifted at everything. Each of us has both strengths and weaknesses.

As a leader, one of my primary roles is properly placing each team member in the right spot. When there is a challenge that needs to be met in our church, I always want to believe that God has already given us the leader we need with the gifts to meet the challenge. We just need to discover His plan! I also want to help my team members identify and employ their spiritual gifts, and recognize the areas where they are not gifted.

Some are gifted speakers; some are not. Some are gifted administrators; some are not. Some are gifted counselors; some are not. If I continue to try to get a team member to excel in an area where they simply aren't gifted, it's like trying to drive a square peg into a round hole. It's going to be hard. It's going to hurt. It's going to damage. Frankly, it's not happening. I owe each person proper placement. I tell them this all the time. They know that's my goal— for them and for the organization. Often, moving a team member to a spot on the team that better matches their gifts can allow them to flourish instead of flounder. It's my responsibility to help them find that proper placement—before I consider releasing them.

Prayer

We owe our team members our prayers. I may not see the future clearly, but God does. One of the most important things a leader can do is to take leadership matters to Him in prayer. I pray for my team members. Systematically, I try to pray over my calendar each day. I look over yesterday's calendar and thank Him for what He did through others. I also look at today's calendar and pray for the interactions I will have, taking the opportunity to pray for each person's family, thank God for their strengths, and ask Him to help them in areas where I think they need to grow. I cannot overstate how much God has used these prayers.

Hundreds of times over the years, I have sat down to speak with an individual about a perceived blind spot or a situation in their lives or work, when God has prompted their hearts to bring the issue up! It turned out that God had been speaking to them. There are God moments you will never understand unless you have been there.

It's a great honor and responsibility that God uses my prayers in the lives of my employees. And I believe He is counting on me to intercede for them. I still stand amazed at that truth, and try to remember to always pray for team members more than I critique or criticize them. If you take one thing from this book, let it be that!

KNOWING WHEN TO RELEASE

As I mentioned earlier, releasing someone from the team should always be a last resort. There are lots of other options. That being said, sometimes releasing an employee is the last option open to us. How do we know when it's time to release someone? There are three scenarios in which releasing someone is probably not only the only option, but also the best option for us, for the team member, and the organization. I mentioned the Four C's earlier. No matter how great a job we have done on the front end when hiring, and no matter how honest we have been with a team member, sometimes issues just don't improve over time and must be dealt with.

Character Issues

Sometimes, even after several conversations, coachings, and reviews, an employee's behavior remains a challenge. Over the years, I have consistently told my team members that I can help them grow and develop, as long as they want to do that. We can be on the same team for a long time, as long as they are teachable and coachable. On the flip side, when a team member ceases to grow and refuses to change problematic behavior, continues to be defensive, or refuses to step up and meet the standards even after being moved to a new spot on the team, well, releasing them becomes the only option.

Capacity Issues

Even the best leaders have a capacity lid. In the book of Exodus, Moses reached his:

> The next day Moses took his seat to serve as judge for the people, and they stood around him from morning till evening. When his father-in-law saw all that Moses was doing for the people, he said, "What is this you are doing for the people? Why do you alone sit as judge, while all these people stand around you from morning till evening?" (Ex. 18:13–14)

Jethro, Moses' father-in-law, recognized that Moses had failed to empower other leaders in the camp. He was frustrating everyone. He was wearing everyone out! Moses had become the bottleneck for the entire organization. He didn't see it. Most leaders don't. We can't see our own capacity lids; we need other people to help us recognize them, just as Jethro called out Moses' limitations.

The great news is that Moses demonstrated true leadership by listening to Jethro and making the changes that needed to be made. In response to Jethro's coaching, Moses selected and empowered leaders with various levels of capacity and responsibility. He placed leaders over groups of a thousand, hundred, fifty, and ten. After the changes were made, everyone felt the difference, and Israel prospered at a new level. In doing this, Moses proved that he had a higher capacity lid than anyone thought—because he empowered leaders to carry out God's vision along with Him!

On the flip side, had Moses refused to listen, or had he procrastinated in taking Jethro's advice for too long, he could have eventually lost his right to lead the movement. If he wasn't able to lead the entire movement, he may have been put in charge of a thousand, or a hundred, or fifty, or ten. Everyone has a different capacity lid, and the sooner we realize it, the better off we'll all be.

When we have addressed capacity issues, only to be met with resistance or a lack of ability to change, it's time to make a bigger change. An employee may need to simply be moved to a different seat on the bus, where there's a different capacity lid. Just because they can't lead the whole thing doesn't mean they can't lead part of it. They may be a leader of fifty or ten or two. But after we've moved them once like this, the next failure to perform should probably result in releasing them from the team.

How do we know when someone has reached his or her capacity lid? When tension begins to rise. We'll see a rapid increase in a team member's personal tension: stress, anxiety, frustration, whining, and the like are probably good signs that they are approaching their maximum capacity. Have you ever had someone working for you who seemed fine for months or even years, and then all of a sudden a new tension appeared between you? This could be anything, but could also be a telltale sign of a capacity issue, and it deserves investigation.

A team is only as strong as its weakest link. The longer an employee remains the weak link, the more difficult it becomes for that person, for us, and for the organization. Things get tense. As long as an employee is operating at or above their capacity lid, they are going to be overwhelmed, frustrated, and discouraged. The best thing for them and the organization is to try out a spot on the team that is not above their capacity, or release them and allow them to go somewhere else where they can feel like they are winning again! We owe them that.

Chemistry Issues

When I am thinking of hiring someone, I try to visualize what my first emotion is going to be when I look up from my office and see that person standing at the door. Will I be glad to see this person standing there, or will I think to myself: *Oh, man, not them again.* Let's be honest; we hope everyone gets to heaven, but there are just some people we're hoping won't have a mansion close to ours! (You've got to admit—that's funny.)

If I lack the relational chemistry needed to really do life with a team member, I'm probably not going to invest in them the way they need to be invested in. I'm going to have a hard time spending lots of time with them, which means I probably won't love them the way they need to be loved! Sometimes we don't realize it until we make a hire, but a person is just not a fit on our team. When that is the case, they need to be released sooner than later. Chemistry is not anyone's fault. It's just a reality. When chemistry is not there, we owe it to a team member to acknowledge it. It needs to be a relational fit for their benefit, for our benefit, and the benefit of the organization. If it's sucking the life out of the vision, we need to deal with it.

Calling Issues

Sometimes a team member is just not driven to go where we're going or pay the price everyone else is willing to pay. Every team member should have a WIT (Whatever It Takes) attitude to get the vision accomplished. In years of ministry, I have found that some team members want to be part of a winning team, but they don't want to pay the price of winning. From time to time we would have someone who thought it would be "cool" to work for a church. Then we'd give them the job, and they'd realize that they would have to work harder there than anywhere they had ever worked! They were just not willing to go there. This is a calling issue! If they are not called, they will either limit themselves and the organization by what they are willing to give, or they will become the bottleneck. Neither is healthy.

In conversations with those we hire, we need to be clear on the front end about what's required for the position. I have always said if they can be talked out of it, they weren't called in the first place! Sometimes good people need help from a spiritual leader who is willing to say, "I just don't think you're called to do this."

THE RIGHT WAY TO LET SOMEONE GO

It is possible to do the right thing but do it the wrong way. When releasing someone, it's important to both do the right thing and do it the right way. So don't procrastinate. Don't put this off. When you recognize someone is not working out, and you refuse to do anything about it, you become part of the problem. Once the decision has been made, act and act quickly. What does this look like? How do we let someone go?

Keep It One-on-One

There's no need for a committee or a group of people to be in this meeting. The employee usually won't act as defensively if this meeting is just with you. This also preserves their dignity. Remember, we always owe this person grace—especially if it's over an issue that's out of their control, like chemistry.

Pick the right time. Schedule these types of meetings for the end of the day when most of the other staff members are leaving the office. That way the employee doesn't have to come out of the meeting and try to act like everything's fine, or even worse, make a scene because they're hurting.

Use the Right Tone

There's no need for finger pointing or accusations. There's no need for yelling or screaming. There's no need to get personal. Schedule this meeting after you have had time to cool down from any slights that may have occurred. Never release someone in a heated moment. This meeting is about protecting the vision. Tell them that. Believe that.

Don't Beat Around the Bush

This doesn't need to be a long meeting. Don't chitchat or make small talk once the meeting begins. Small talk could be viewed as superficial or hypocritical. Both of you probably know what this meeting is about, so don't beat around the bush.

Start with the Positive.

This employee hasn't done everything wrong. They've made some positive contributions. God has no doubt used them in some way to make the organization better. Thank the employee for saying yes in the first place to their position. Thank them for their hard work. Talk about the things they've done to add value.

Be Specific

Tell them exactly why this release is happening. Be gentle but be specific. There's no need for a laundry list of what they've done wrong. Just pick one or two overarching reasons why this is not going to work out. Be honest with them. Talk about fit. Talk about the vision. Talk about what's best for them and the organization.

Acknowledge Your Pain

Let the employee know that you have lost sleep over this decision. Tell them this is not easy for you. Tell them this hurts you. Tell them you love them (we should, you know). Tell them you hate having this discussion as much as they do, but that your first responsibility is to this organization, no matter how difficult it is. Acknowledge their pain as well. Let them know you realize there have been frustrating times as of late. You know things have been difficult for them. This will make things more difficult in the short run, but better in the long run. Let them know that you believe this move can relieve some of the frustration and tension they have been feeling lately. In the end, both of you will be better for this. You should really believe that.

Put Everything in Writing

Good paper makes good friends. Everything needs to be on paper in terms of an exit agreement. We need to stipulate in writing, in general terms, why each exit is happening, when an employee's last day will be (even if it's today), and how long and how much that person will be paid.

Offer the High Road

Tell them you would love to still be able to speak positively about them when you leave this meeting. Talk about how you would like to handle the communication of the employee's exit from the team. You might say something like this:

> From the way I see it today, when we leave this room, we have two choices: I would love to take the high road. I would love for us to just agree that it's time to part ways in a Christian manner. I would love for us to speak positively of each other, including what we say on social media.
>
> If you are willing to take that high road, I would like to offer a generous severance as part of our exit agreement [probably up to ninety days]. However, if you decide you can't do this, and you take the low road and begin to run the organization down or run me down to others, all bets are off, and it will terminate that agreement. With that in mind, are you willing to take the high road?

I know all of this may sound a bit harsh. But remember: we owe them grace, honesty, clarity, and accountability, proper placement, and prayer! All of these things are crucial in this moment. We cannot mince words here. We need to set clear, healthy boundaries for the relationship going forward. We also must preserve and protect what matters: the vision!

End the Meeting Graciously

To my recollection, I have ended every single one of these conversations with a handshake and even a hug! I have prayed for and with the team member. I've told that person I loved them, and I meant it. If our hearts are right, this is a difficult moment for both the leader and the team member, but we have moved forward so that the vision could win the day.

How do people usually respond in a conversation like this? Frankly lots of ways. Don't get caught up in how they will respond. Just focus on doing the right thing the right way and trust God with the outcome. Don't worry about who's going to be upset about the decision, or who else might leave. You have to trust that God will protect you and your organization. Do the right thing and trust God with the rest. That's called *faith*.

 Do the right thing and trust God with the rest. That's called *faith*.

Remember this: short-term pain brings long-term gain. The organization and the vision are going to win because of these hard decisions. Keeping this mind helps us do the tough thing. Can I encourage you? I've not had a single one of these types of conversations end up looking like an episode of *Jerry Springer*. It's never gotten that crazy. These conversations have never been as terrible as the scenarios I have imagined ahead of time. I actually believe Satan likes to make us think about worst-case scenarios so he can keep us from pursuing the vision God has for us and our organizations! Don't allow this to happen to you.

ONE FIRE AWAY

So many of us think we're one great hire away from new growth in our companies. But I have actually run across many churches and organizations that are just one *fire* away from new growth! Many organizations could collectively breathe a sigh of relief if one team member who isn't fitting well was released.

Here's another confession in this book, and depending on your sports loyalties, you may have a big problem with it: I grew up in the great state of Alabama, and I am a lifelong University of Alabama football fan. Judge me if you must, but it's in my blood. I cried when the great coach Paul "Bear" Bryant passed away. Not kidding. I have met Nick Saban, head football coach for the University of Alabama, on numerous occasions. He knows about football, and that means he knows about how people act on teams. I once heard Coach Saban make the statement in an interview that "mediocre people don't like high achievers and high achievers don't like mediocre people."[1]

Wow. I agree with that. I have been around athletic teams my whole life. I have seen this dynamic in play on many teams. Great athletes love the challenge of competing for a starting spot against other great athletes. They know this pushes them to be better. They love to be challenged. They love to be surrounded with greatness. However, great football players' number one pet peeve is having someone on the team who doesn't give his best effort. They struggle with players who can't get the job done. They hate having someone on the team that can't pull his weight.

On the flip side, mediocre players love to be on the roster with great players. See, mediocre players who don't give great effort or play at a high level can still win rings and championships, and receive the fame without ever doing anything significant themselves! Mediocre players often like to hide on a great team. They like to win without ever having to score a touchdown or even make a tackle. But a team is only as strong as its weakest link. Mediocrity is a disease, and the disease is contagious. It's like a cancer; if your organization is to live, the cancer needs to be removed. Otherwise it will spread, and it will kill. This is that serious!

> Mediocrity is a disease, and the
> disease is contagious.

If you're not yet convinced, here's one final motivation to have courageous conversations with team members about their performance or support of the vision. A leader loses credibility every day a mediocre team member stays around. The great players on the team know who the mediocre player is. Most everyone can identify the weak link. Every day we tolerate them and don't deal with their issues, people begin to wonder: *Does our leader recognize what's going on? Are they oblivious to the weak link?* Courageous conversations build credibility within a team. Dealing with mediocrity earns respect. The team knows that we are there for them, to make the tough calls and place the vision's health above personal comfort, including our own.

In My Journal

► If I were starting the organization today, would I re-hire everyone who is currently on our team? Why or why not? If not, who?

► Right now, if I had to write down the name of someone who is at risk of being released from our organization, who would it be? Why do I think so?

► Do I really believe that releasing someone from our organization could also benefit them? Why or why not?

► What could potentially keep me from releasing someone who needs to be released?

TEN

GETTING BACK ON TRACK

So here's a question some of you have been waiting on for the entire book. What do we do when we look up and realize the vision has drifted? How do we transition an entire organization back on track when it has lost its way? I've had to do it, and it wasn't easy, but we pulled it off! I'll share with you how in the pages that follow.

A few years ago, when I recognized the need for some changes in our church's culture, I knew I was up against a great task. No one likes change, after all, unless it's their idea. This was our challenge as I saw it: For about a decade, there's been an ongoing debate about whether a church should be *attractional* or *missional*. Basically the two words describe the church's paradigm for reaching new people. Should we ask people to come gather with us, or should we go to them and de-emphasize the large gathering? To me that argument has always been a little foolish, because I believe the answer is, both! The church should invite people into our gatherings, whether it's in a home or a large building, for worship and community—then commission them to live Christ's love in our community, nation, and world!

I was concerned that our church had grown too comfortable with an *attractional* method of reaching people. In that model, churches invite people to come check things out in their building, in hopes that they might experience life change there. But too many churches want everyone to come, even if they don't "go" out into the world and carry out Christ's work. Honestly, I could see our church headed down this road.

I don't have time to get into all of the changes I thought we would need to make to become more missional. That's a different book. But I can tell you—we knew we would have to revamp and change a lot about our church to get back on track.

I knew our mission and mission statement would need to be examined and potentially modified. I knew our small-group model and branding would need to change. Our worship services would need to be examined and potentially reshaped. The question was *how*? How was I going to steer everyone in a new direction *and* preserve the vision? And how could I do it without blowing everything up?

 The right thing done the wrong way
still produces the wrong results.

In fact, I decided to write here on the issue of change because I've already seen too many leaders go off to a conference, then come back and stand up at a staff meeting (or worse yet, a worship service) and say: "Hey, I've been to a conference. God spoke to me, and we're changing everything, starting today!" That is a great way to bring down the house.

John Maxwell likes to quote, "He that thinketh he leadeth, and hath no one following, is only taking a walk."[1] I'll just add: he may be taking a walk off the plank!

What do we do when we realize that certain programs, approaches, methods, or strategies aren't working anymore? What if they aren't effective in helping us accomplish our mission any longer? How do we lead our organization through change?

I'm happy to say that in our church's case, I was able to lead us through some pretty significant cultural shifts without splitting the church. In fact, we took the lion's share of people with us on this journey! I want to share with you how we did it, and give you the courage to make the transitions you need to make to keep your organization effective in accomplishing its vision.

MODEL THE WAY

Since behavior is more caught than taught, I was going to have to start with myself if we were going to be successful in this transition. I was going to need to model the way. I would need to hold my leaders accountable to modeling the way as well. Our big shift would require not only cultural changes but changes in the behaviors and schedules of our staff. I couldn't hold them accountable to things I wasn't willing to do.

What did this look like practically? If I wanted our church to go where people were going out into the world, then, as a pastor, I had to get out of the church building and go live life where unchurched people lived! I had to take the church to the community. I joined my local Rotary Club. I volunteered to coach my son's football team. I started spending less time in the church building and more time with people disconnected from the church. As a leader, I had to model the way.

The same is true for all of us. For example, most pastors I know say they believe in Sunday school or small groups. Just don't ask them if they actually belong to a class or group. The answer is often, "Who, me? Wow, I just don't have time for that with my schedule." Pastors, if we're too busy, why would we think other people would be able to do what we ask them to do? Most church members work more than fifty hours a week, then volunteer for a few hours on top of that! If we can't or won't do it, we shouldn't expect anyone else to do it. Period. If we are a manager of a company who employs salespeople, and we expect them to get out of the office and sell, then we should as well. If we want our organizations to exemplify honesty and loyalty, then we should be honest and loyal. Leaders go first. Leaders model the way, especially during times of transition.

SEEK OUTSIDE HELP

Have you ever had an *Aha!* moment? I had one just prior to our church's time of transition. Almost every church I had ever seen transition successfully appeared to have sought counsel and brought in outside help. They brought in a coach or consultant to help their teams work through the issues, identify the problems and challenges, and navigate into the future. I am a strong advo-cate of bringing in people from the outside to help an organization transition successfully. (In fact, it's one of the focuses of my current ministry, Courage to Lead.[2])

Our church invested a large chunk of resources that year to bring in a series of coaches, consultants, and leaders from churches I thought we could learn from. Keep in mind, our goal wasn't to "copycat" what everyone else was doing, but to learn from them and contextualize those lessons for our environment, tailored to fit within the framework of our vision. I allowed these leaders to teach our staff and facilitate candid conversations about our strengths, weaknesses, and challenges. They helped our staff begin to identify, embrace, and become stakeholders in the transitions we needed to make.

BE PATIENT

Patience is a virtue, but here's the challenge: I've rarely met a patient leader. As leaders, by our very nature, we like to move fast. We love the thrill of going Mach 5 with our hair on fire. We love change. For leaders, change is like a drug. And we like to change things—a lot!

For these reasons, one of the primary mistakes leaders make in enacting change is trying to do it too quickly. We are not patient with people. We might take some time on the front end to pray about a decision, process it, talk it over with a few key staff. Then we walk out and announce the change and just expect everyone to get fired up about it without having the luxury of the journey we have taken. They might embrace the change with their mouths, but not in their heads or their hearts.

When we are enacting change, we don't simply want compliance. We want conviction. We want them to believe in the change as strongly as we do. But it takes time to make someone a stakeholder of change.

The goal of our church during our time of transition was simply to move up the scale of change each year, not to change it within a year. I know we think that if we don't make the change quickly we'll be behind. But the goal of our church's transition was to go on a two-to-three year spiritual journey, whereby everyone in our church would eventually embrace the transition to a missional focus. Let me tell you more about what that journey looked like.

START WITH THE LEADERS

As the leaders go, the rest of the organization will go. So first of all, we should never surprise our leaders with change. It's a mistake to announce big change in a full staff meeting, or God forbid, from a stage or platform, without first having the support from key leaders. First of all, this is a good way to get fired! But even if that's not on the table, if we try to enact change without support from key leaders, our attempts at change are dead in the water before we get started. Instead, we need to have lots of smaller meetings before *the* meeting where we announce the change to everyone. Plan these meetings by asking yourself some simple questions: *Who needs to be stakeholder in this before we go public with this? Who has influence?*

Who will people run to when I announce the change? Who will be put in a position where they might need to defend the change? Or defend me? We should seek to get those key players on board first. Leaders need to be able to look in our eyes up close, and to hear our hearts before anyone else does.

In my ministry, I have always begun talking about change in many conversations, in multiple settings, and in small circles—even one-on-one. Life happens over meals, coffee, and in honest meetings with small groups. Meeting with key leaders privately allows them to process, give feedback, and even push back in a healthy, vision-focused way. Like everyone else, they need time to process and understand what we're doing and why we're doing it, and understand how we're going to do it. This will put them in a much better position to support and even defend a decision once it has gone public

In these conversations, some key people will actually make us think about things we had not previously thought about. They will help us see landmines and stumbling blocks we might not have seen. In these meetings I always ask the leaders to think about what we've talked about and promise that I will circle back around with them. I give them time to process it all and then follow up later. Sometimes I just give them my cell number and tell them to call me if they have any questions before we go public with the change. In the case of our big change at Mountain Lake, I did not move forward from this phase until I had support from *all* the key influencers in our church. After all, if two-dozen people can't rally around something, what are the odds an entire organization will? Zero.

As I mentioned earlier, I am a big fan of leadership retreats in these cases. They give us opportunity to do life with our key people, and the time to spell out in detail any changes we feel led to make. Usually at the end of a retreat, most of the leaders are on the same page and excited about the future.

After the staff and key leaders are on board, and all of them are stakeholders in the changes we are going to attempt, it is time to go public. There is a lot of work involved in slowing down to enact change this way. But the slower approach definitely pays off. You'll encounter less complaining and criticism and more unity and synergy around the vision. That's what we want!

Once change has begun, *stay close to the leaders.* Have you ever heard of distance decay? With leaders, it's more like distance destruction. Leaders drift faster than followers. Most of the time leaders are hard-charging, entrepreneurial, type-A personalities. If they don't know the vision, they will make one up. If your approach is simply to plug a leader in and move on, you are making a big mistake. There's a big difference between leader placement and leader development. This is even more the case when it comes to vision.

 There's a big difference between leader
placement and leader development.

SHOW THE BENEFIT

From our key people to the entire organization, everyone needs to know why change is good for them. Think back to our earlier conversation about the *why* and the *what*. Remembering *why* we do *what* we do always creates passion. Too many leaders forget this principle when communicating change. They begin talking about "doing what's best for the organization." No one is motivated by that speech.

In communicating change, we always need to start with *why* the change will be better. It begins with sharing our hearts. The more we're transparent, the more we talk about the things that bother us and about the tension we feel with the way things have been, the more open people will be. Our team members need to know we've prayed about the change. We've sought counsel about it. They need to know that these changes aren't just the latest good idea. If we demonstrate that we have wrestled with it, they will be more prepared to make whatever sacrifices the change might require.

Our team members need to know that we have thought about them in this process. They need to hear that we have calculated the cost, not just for the organization, but for them personally! We need to be able to say with integrity that in the long run, the change is better for the people, not just for the bottom line. Then the challenge is to communicate the proposed changes in such a way that we point out the benefits to everyone involved.

How will this change produce the results everyone wants? Even if the change will be difficult in the short run, how will it benefit all of us in the long run? Why should each team member embrace the change? Last but not least, how will this benefit the organization and help us be more successful in our vision? Frankly, this is the most important element, but in communicating change, it should be the last element we talk about. If team members know *first* that we have thought about them, care about them, and have developed a plan to change with them in mind, they will more quickly embrace the change and vision. Leaders touch the heart before they ask for a hand. It's dangerous to skip over this simple but powerful principle.

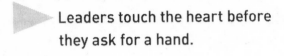

Leaders touch the heart before they ask for a hand.

GO PUBLIC

As you can see, our church had done almost a year of "under the hood" vision casting and leadership development, *before* we went public with proposed changes. Then, finally, I stood up on a Sunday morning and shared my love for our church, while being transparent about some of my struggles with the church. That was the time to explain the changes I felt needed to happen. On top of that, I was able to tell them that I was not the only one who felt this way, but our finance team, advisory team, our staff, and over one hundred key leaders in our church had all been in the loop before today, and were 100 percent behind the changes. Who could argue with that? Few did. But our job wasn't done. We still knew this was going to be a long process.

We kicked off a new six-week series that weekend at church called "The Bold Life," which sought to help people personalize the missional approach and galvanize everyone around it. We had every small group in our church talking about the same subject during those six weeks, all throughout our community. Even if there was pushback in that group, we already had every small group leader on board with the change, and we trusted them to share the vision and garner support.

Did we get complete support from everyone in our church on the changes? What do you think? Even Jesus didn't get complete support. If we're waiting on that, we'll never make a decision! Did some people get upset? You bet they did. Did some people leave our church? Yes. Our goal in making big decisions at our church has never been to "hold on" to everybody. We just want to take most of our people with us. Leadership is not taking people where they want to go. It's taking people where they need to go! The good news is that the loss was so minimal that very few even noticed it. It didn't faze our leaders because we had prepared them for this. We equipped them to manage change and even conflict. In the church, that's part of discipleship.

After we went public with some of the transitions that would better facilitate our vision, we didn't just stop after a six-week series of discussions. We kept talking about it every week. We constantly reinforced the message in our leadership meetings and training materials, as well as from the platform on the weekends at our church. We wanted everyone to get the message that this was not just a new program that would come and go. This was a new way of thinking, being, and doing in our church. We were going to be different moving forward, and it was obvious to everyone. We were committed to these changes.

It's tempting for leaders to move quickly from one good idea to the next. We read an article, attend a conference, or hear a speaker, and we might get fired up and change everything, only to move on to another new thing the next year. Many leaders have conditioned their organizations to expect this. Some of their team members may come to realize that if they just sit still and refuse to move, the leader will eventually move on to the next big thing. As leaders, we must *never change simply for the sake of change.* When we enact change in our organization, it should always be intentional and have everything to do with the vision.

HOLD PEOPLE ACCOUNTABLE

Remember: clarity allows accountability. I would also add that success *requires* accountability. In consulting with leaders, I have found that many of them do a good job of being crystal clear with their vision and the changes that need to be happening in the organization. But that doesn't stop some of the other influencers in the organization from digging their heels in and simply refusing to change. When we seek to enact change, communication is not the only critical element; we also need a plan to hold our leaders accountable.

During our transition, we at Mountain Lake realized that change was moving slower in some areas, simply because some of our small group leaders were trying to fly under the radar and refusing to budge! The best approach to this was to communicate clearly that we were not only going to show the pathway to success for our small groups, but we were going to hold our leaders accountable for the changes.

We let them know that we would be sitting down with them

six months from now to assess the success of the group and how it had moved in the new direction we felt led toward. Once again, it was amazing to see what happened as we raised the bar and promised to hold leaders accountable. Slowly, they either aligned with the new vision or they fired themselves by stepping down. We were at peace with either decision, but it was important to us that at least 90 percent of our groups own this new vision within three years.

CHANGE WHAT YOU CELEBRATE

You'll remember that what gets celebrated gets done. What does your organization celebrate? Attendance? Giving? Revenue? Budgets? Buildings? Hard work? Sacrifice? Working long hours to get the job done? What we celebrate communicates what we value. So if we want to move the organization in a new direction, we need to figure out how to celebrate any and every small win that takes us there. Through e-mails, announcements, videos, and personal stories, we can show the desired result happening in the lives of real people. We can tell a story and allow others to model the way! This is compelling. This is attractive. People want to be part of something that's working. So the question we need to wrestle with is, how often and in how many ways could you begin to celebrate what you want to see happen in your entire organization? Go look for it. Mine for it. It's there. You just have to find it, even if it's a diamond in the rough. Even if it's just one person, champion them. Tell their story. What gets celebrated gets done.

STAY THE COURSE

Change is difficult. Enacting change not only requires a lot of courage; it requires clarity and commitment. Most of all, change requires patience. It takes time for the shepherd to lead all the sheep into the fold safely. Of course it's a challenge, but never give up on a change because it's difficult. God-inspired change brings new movement in the direction of the vision. If we can keep our eyes on the vision during these long, tense seasons of change, we'll see success. "Let us not become weary in doing good, for at the proper time we will reap a harvest if we do not give up" (Gal. 6:9).

It's a fact: change is difficult. But here's another fact: change is worth it. When you're trying to lead your organization through change, there will be times when the pain is so difficult you want to give up. I plead with you not to do it. Don't ever leave just because it's hard. Don't retreat with your tail between your legs. Don't quit after a big loss. Don't quit just because someone else thinks you should.

When should you quit? When is the best time to step down? When there's absolutely no reason to leave. You leave when things are on a high note. Leave when everything's clicking. Leave when there's no drama—no one expects you to leave, when no one wants you to leave. (We'll talk more about passing the baton in the last chapter.) Stay the course until things are going well, and *only then* think about what's next. Once you've begun a change, it is your responsibility to see it through to the next high note.

In My Journal

▶ What changes need to be made in our culture?

▶ Who would I begin with and how would I start gaining
   support of change in our organization's culture?

▶ When and how am I tempted to give up on the vision?

▶ Take some time here to map out a rough draft of the
   transition process to get things back on track. Include
   key people, events, and meetings.

PLEASING THE RIGHT AUDIENCE

Every day we live on the stage of life. We know people are watching. We perform. We work. We act. We bring our best effort and skill. We want to make an impact—to be discovered, noticed, or even famous. We want to have a platform. We want to be recognized as successful, and to hear the world's applause. Usually we're doing what we're doing with a particular audience in mind. One of the most eye-opening things we can discover about ourselves as leaders is *which* audience we're trying to please, and why.

Who are you trying to please? *Why* are you doing what you're doing? Do you have a chip on your shoulder trying to prove someone wrong? Or are you competing with someone or another organization? Are you trying to please all your church members? Your key givers? The board? A committee? Stakeholders? Maybe you're just trying to prove something to yourself. Or perhaps you're terrified of failing, and you feel like you owe it to yourself to win.

People pleasing and leadership can exist in a great tension. On one level, leaders must understand that people usually buy into *us* before they buy into the vision. People need to like us. We need to like people. As leaders, we always need to have our eyes on the people we lead and our ears to the ground, willing to hear about their challenges and concerns. Shepherds need to know the condition of our flocks. We also need the support of the people we lead.

On the flip side, there's a difference between pleasing people and being a people pleaser. While it's important to be sensitive to others, pleasing people can never be our most important responsibility. At the end of the day, we must choose to please God first and foremost. He has called us and placed us where we are for a reason. That reason is His vision for our life and our organization. He is ultimately the only audience we must please at all costs.

Many biblical leaders had to make this critical choice. One such leader was Esther of the Bible. What's crazy about Esther is that she didn't necessarily want to be a leader. But early on in the story, it is clear Esther had one good thing going for her: she was easy on the eyes. In fact, she was beautiful. People noticed. The king of Persia noticed. After a king-sponsored beauty pageant, Esther was thrust into a leadership role as the queen of Persia. At that point the king didn't even know that Esther was a Jew. Then, with the help of the evil Haman, he played a part in setting into place a sequence of events that would basically mean mass genocide against the Jews, Esther's people.

Esther had to make a choice: (1) keep her Jewish roots a secret and allow her people to perish while saving her own neck; or (2) risk it all, let her secret out, approach the king, and plead for her people. Then Mordecai, Esther's cousin and former guardian, issued a strong challenge:

> For if you remain silent at this time, relief and deliverance for the Jews will arise from another place, but you and your father's family will perish. And who knows but that you have come to your royal position for such a time as this? (Est. 4:14)

Mordecai was saying: "Esther, what if God has placed you in this difficult situation for His eternal purposes? What if you take the easy way, but it's not God's way? What if God has placed you in this position of influence to protect His vision for His people?" Believe it or not, I think this is a choice you and I make almost every week. We choose to take the easy way—the way that seems less awkward and less uncomfortable for us—or we choose to do what we feel pleases God. Whether we realize it or not, God has a calling for our lives. He has gifted us for a purpose. He has placed us where we are in leadership for such a time as this. Will we choose to please Him regardless of the perceived cost?

In Esther's case, after fasting and praying about it, she did the difficult thing. Regardless of what the king would think, or what all of Persia would think, Esther decided to honor God and trust Him with the outcome. She literally said, "If I perish, I perish" (Est. 4:16). In other words, "I'm going to do what I feel like God wants me to do, and I'm going to trust Him whatever the outcome, whatever the cost."

You might know what happened next: Esther appeared before the king and pleaded with him. He could not have shocked her more with his response. He granted her grace and favor and set into motion a new turn of events that saved the entire Jewish race, and reestablished them as one of the most powerful nations on the planet:

> In every province and in every city to which the edict of the king came, there was joy and gladness among the Jews, with feasting and celebrating. And many people of other nationalities became Jews because fear of the Jews had seized them. (Est. 8:17)

By choosing to serve God above all, she actually saved herself and her people. Leadership requires an incredible amount of courage. Sometimes we have to do what's best for people even when it doesn't please all of the people. We find this same pattern throughout Scripture.

When Jesus came along, He didn't please everyone. He didn't even try to please everyone. At times He seems to have intentionally antagonized the Pharisees: "You snakes! You brood of vipers! How will you escape being condemned to hell?" (Matt. 23:33). Try saying that to your board and see what happens! Those kinds of statements won't win friends and influence people. They could get you run out of town, or maybe even killed. That's what they did to Jesus. So if Jesus knew this, why would He speak to other leaders in such a polarizing way? Because Jesus knew these religious leaders had their own agenda for His life. They wanted to try to get Him to be something He wasn't. They wanted to hijack the vision that God had given Him. Jesus loved everyone, but he loved God first and foremost, and He wouldn't allow anyone or anything to hijack the vision.

Jesus didn't come to please everyone. He came to please His heavenly Father and fulfill His purpose. He was focused on completing the task God had given Him. He was secure in His own identity, and confident in His calling. He recognized that His greatest responsibility was seeing the original vision through to completion. He was accountable to God to stay the course.

Two thousand years later, you have the same responsibility. You won't ever please everybody. That shouldn't be the goal. People pleasing can be a slippery slope, and it can endanger the vision. Instead, believe that God has placed you where you are in your sphere of leadership for a reason. You are here "for such a time as this."

> If it comes down to a choice between pleasing people and pleasing God, choose the latter.

Choose courageous conversations. Choose courageous decisions. Choose to say the difficult thing. Choose conflict over artificial harmony. Choose to take a stand, and to refuse to be bullied by criticism from the peanut gallery.

The apostle Paul certainly faced criticism for his way of spreading the gospel. Here's how he responded:

> Obviously, I'm not trying to win the approval of people, but of God. If pleasing people were my goal, I would not be Christ's servant. (Gal. 1:10 NLT)

I'm not saying we should be arrogant and unwilling to listen to people. I'm not saying we shouldn't be accountable as leaders. I've had an amazing group of people surround me during my time as lead pastor of Mountain Lake, and I gave them permission to speak into my life. They had permission to say the difficult things to me, and to help me see my blind spots. They challenged me and challenged my thinking on things. But I gave these people permission for three very specific reasons: they love God, they love the vision, and they also love me!

In the chapter on vision hijackers, we discussed the difference between those who criticize for ulterior motives, and those who critique out of love. These are people who I know have our church's best interests at heart; but I also know they have my best interest at heart. Even if they have to say something I might initially find offensive or upsetting, I know it's only because they love me and they love our church, and they want what's best for both.

THE DIFFERENCE BETWEEN A
CRITIQUE AND A CRITICISM

There's a difference between a *critique* and a *criticism*. People who meet the above criteria have permission to critique me now and again. I need to hear that. I need to be sharpened, to grow, and to hear the truth spoken in love to me. It's healthy to have people challenge my thinking on things. Critiques make us better.

Criticism, on the other hand, might come from people who have a critical spirit or an ulterior motive. These people could have an agenda or selfish ambitions. I don't listen to criticisms. Critics usually won't come and talk to me face to face anyway. They will send a letter or e-mail—anonymously, of course. I don't read anonymous e-mails or letters. My assistant filters them and trashes them for me before I even see them. If you are one of my anonymous critics reading this, that could be why I haven't answered you!

Critics in this sense are often cowards. They usually don't practice the process of confrontation found in Matthew 18, which begins with private, loving conversation. In these instances, I often feel like Nehemiah did when he was rebuilding the wall. I just don't have time for it. I'll not be slowed down by it, and I won't allow someone who's got any other agenda beside the vision to dictate my life, ministry, or calling, or to sidetrack this organization.

> I am determined not to be deterred by my critics.
> I hope you will make the same determination.

The most significant decision we can make in this life is the choice to please the right audience. So let me ask you once again: Who are you trying to please? Who or what is driving you? Why do you want to be successful? What does success look like to you?

I don't know what you thought you were signing up for when you signed up for leadership, but allow me to let you in on a secret. Leadership is stressful. Followers make suggestions, but leaders make decisions. Leadership requires wisdom, discernment, courage, and sacrifice. Leadership can be painful. And leaders are often misunderstood. And to add to the stress, leaders are often targets. We always have enemies. Always—no matter how "nice" we are.

Leaders get attacked, and must sometimes stand alone. Leadership can be lonely. Now, who wants to be a leader?

This is why we had better be secure in our callings. We had better believe that God has called us where we are and placed us in our positions. And we must remember *why* we're doing what we're doing. Is it to gain the applause of men or the applause of God? When we keep our eyes on our Creator, we remember that He has called us and given us a vision—a unique destiny to fulfill. We, like Esther, play a critical role in His plan. If we quit or relent, we aren't just quitting on our dream; we are quitting on His dream for us! If we stay true to the vision, no matter the outcome, we are successful in His eyes. Isn't that all that matters?

A FACE IN THE CROWD

As I mentioned earlier, I have always been a big college football fan. This passion goes back to my "glory days" in high school. I was a pretty good football player. I loved it too. I was also the meanest 165-pound defensive end you have ever seen! Man, I miss those glory days!

My dad has never been a huge football fan, but he has always been my number one fan. My mom went to heaven earlier in life, and my dad had to run his own business while playing "soccer mom" at the same time for my sister and me. I don't remember a game I ever played that my dad missed. He was always there cheering me on from the stands.

If you've ever participated in athletics, you know that once you get into the game on the field, a strange dynamic starts. Once the game begins, you usually "zone out" to what's going on up in the stands. The announcer might call your name, and the fans might cheer, but often you're so focused on what you're doing, you don't hear any of it. But even so, there was always one person I wanted to pick out of the crowd and one voice I was always listening for. You guessed it: my dad. In fact, as soon as I took the field before each game, I would scan the crowd looking for him. As I made eye contact with others, they might wave and try to keep my attention, but my eyes moved on. I was on a mission: find my number one fan.

I would find my dad in the crowd, and when my eyes finally found his, his eyes were already on me. When our gazes met, no matter how nervous I was about the game, I felt a new sense of peace and passion. My dad was watching, and I was going to make him proud. When our eyes would meet, my dad would always give me a thumbs-up. That meant he was with me. He believed in me. Now, I could go play!

Many times during a game, when I would make a catch or a great tackle, regardless of what the rest of the crowd was doing, my eyes would jump to one special part of the stands where my dad was seated. Regardless of how everyone else responded to the play, I really only cared about how one person was responding. The only thing more gratifying than the great catch or tackle was to look up and catch my dad celebrating. Sometimes he was high-fiving everyone around him. Sometimes he was screaming and pumping his fists. I would see people congratulate him on his son. I could see him applauding. Every once in a while, I could even read his lips. He was saying: "That's my son! That's my son!" I always played football for an audience of one person: my dad. I might have played somewhat for my own glory, but ultimately I played for his.

In a similar way, as you and I take to the field of leadership, there are lots of spectators in the stands. Their support will rise and fall based on the momentum of the game and the cumulative wins or losses of the season. Most fans will come and go. But there's one fan who never checks out. He never misses a game. His eyes are always on us. He believes in us. He is our heavenly Father.

Sometimes on the heels of a difficult decision or conversation, when I am staggering under the weight of leadership, I literally try to visualize my heavenly Father standing in the crowd. Does He approve of my decision? Of my indecision? How will He respond to what's just happened? I'm looking intently now. How does He feel about what I'm doing? The way I'm playing the game? As my eyes focus on Him, I'm looking to see: Does He approve? Is He applauding? No one else may cheer, but as long as He does, I can do this. I can make it. I can do it again and again, as long as I'm living for an audience of One. If I am pursuing the vision He has given me with every ounce of passion and energy that I have, He is proud of me. Regardless of the scoreboard, as long as I'm giving my best to steward the vision well, He is proud. At the end of the game, His approval is all that matters.

My greatest prayer for our time together is that God would somehow give you the ability to live for an audience of One. I pray that God gives you the ability to find Him in the crowd. He's there. Regardless of whether everyone else is watching or not, He is. He cares. He called you here. He cares more about seeing this vision through than you do. Don't give up on it, and don't give up on

Him. He's cheering for you. I'm cheering for you too, if that helps! I wrote this book because I care about you—about leaders. And leaders who've gone before you are cheering for you too. We all realize what's at stake: this is about God and His vision. And that's why we're mean about the vision.

The writer of Hebrews said it this way:

> Therefore, since we are surrounded by such a great cloud of witnesses, let us throw off everything that hinders and the sin that so easily entangles. And let us run with perseverance the race marked out for us, fixing our eyes on Jesus, the pioneer and perfecter of faith. For the joy set before him he endured the cross, scorning its shame, and sat down at the right hand of the throne of God. Consider him who endured such opposition from sinners, so that you will not grow weary and lose heart. (12:1–3)

We believe God has spoken to us. We can't quit on this before God is done with us. Make a pronouncement right now. You're not going to quit until you know God has accomplished His vision through you. Live to please an audience of One. Don't listen to naysayers or the vision hijackers. Live for His purposes and finish well.

In My Journal

- Who or what drives most of my leadership decisions?
- Do I care too much about what people think? Why or why not?

- ▶ How can I better differentiate the critiques from the criticisms?
- ▶ What adjustments do I need to make in my life to live more for an audience of One?

TWELVE

RELEASING THE VISION TO A NEW LEADER

If you have never considered leaving your post of leadership, you don't need to read the pages that follow. If you never get restless or feel trapped in your position, stop reading. If you never think you'll retire (or die for that matter), you don't need this chapter. If you want the vision to be built around you and then die with you, close the book now. But if you believe the day will come when you will need to pass the baton and release the vision of your organization to another leader, then this chapter was written just for you.

We've agreed that the vision does *not* belong to the leader. The vision always belongs to God. The leader is only a steward, or manager, of the vision. His or her responsibility is to steward that vision under God's leadership, in a way that God desires, for as long as God desires. Therefore, sooner or later, leaders have to recognize that the vision must outlive them for it to be successful long term. A leader's greatest legacy is leaving behind a healthy, thriving organization.

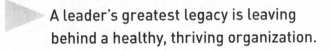

> A leader's greatest legacy is leaving behind a healthy, thriving organization.

A balanced, self-aware leader will realize that the vision eventually needs to be handed over to a new leader. That time came for me last year. After a year of prayer, counsel, and contemplation, I came to the point of realizing that God had in fact laid on my heart a new vision for my life and ministry. This meant that the time would soon come for me to hand the vision God had given me for Mountain Lake Church to a new leader, to lead into the future.

For sixteen years I had devoted my time to both the "little-c" church (Mountain Lake Church in metro Atlanta), and the "big-C" Church (coaching pastors across the country and around the world). At the end of the day, I came to the conclusion that God was calling me to fully focus on the latter. God gave me a new vision of pastoring ten thousand pastors over the next ten years. Pastors need help. Pastors need a friend. Pastors need mentors who are not so caught up in their own ministry drama that they can't be available and accessible to others. Pastors need a safe place to talk through the specific issues that keep them up at night! I'm grateful that God allowed me not only to hear His voice on this matter but also to answer His call.

So God moved me to select my successor, hand off the baton of the vision to a new leader, and ride off into the sunset to pursue the new vision He had given me. My greatest prayer now is that the vision God gave me for Mountain Lake nearly two decades ago not only outlives my leadership, but thrives in my absence! If you think about it, all pastors are interim pastors. Every leader is an interim leader. What does an interim do? Pave the way for the next leader.

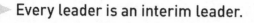 **Every leader is an interim leader.**

Leadership succession is one of the great challenges of any organization—especially for churches. Founding and long-tenured pastors have historically not done so well with successful successions.

My friends William Vanderbloemen and Warren Bird describe the most common approach to succession this way: "Sadly, the story across thousands of churches is all too common: a wonderful pastor moves to another church or retires. The church takes a long time to find a replacement. The successor doesn't last long. The church is off-kilter for a protracted time. Sometimes it never regains its former momentum and health."[1]

In their book *Next: Pastoral Succession That Works,* they go on to give valuable research and counsel regarding how pastors can best steward the vision beyond themselves. Here is one of their conclusions:

> Among senior pastors of megachurches (weekly worship attendance of 2,000 or more adults, youth, and children) according to Leadership Network research, 1 in 5 (22%) are founders and 4 in 5 (78%) are successors. Founders have served on average 19 years and are age 53; successors have served 14 years and are age 52. The message behind these facts is clear: succession is an inevitable issue for pastors and churches. The time to face that reality and to plan for it is now.[2]

There is no success without successful succession! This is why one of the most important decisions I have made in my professional life was the decision to select and empower the new leader that would steward the vision beyond me. I knew that if I did this correctly, the vision would outlive me. If I did this the wrong way, well . . . I think you can guess the rest. In the sections that follow, I'll tell you how to release the vision to the leader who comes after you—at least this is how I did it.

LEAVE ON A HIGH NOTE

We spoke earlier about not quitting when things are looking grim. The correlation is also true: if we have hopes of handing the vision off in a healthy fashion, then the vision needs to be healthy when we hand it off. We don't leave because things are difficult. We don't leave because of criticism, because we're tired, or because it's not fun. We leave because God reveals a new vision. Only cowardly, unhealthy leaders leave when things are bad. If we quit and hand an unhealthy vision over to another leader, it's poor stewardship on our part. Remember Jesus' parable of the talents in Matthew 25? Each servant is entrusted with different levels of "talent." Regardless of what they're given, each of them has the same responsibility: investing well what had been entrusted to them and presenting a healthy return on investment when the master returned.

I felt the same responsibility with Mountain Lake Church. I wanted to leave it in the very best shape possible: emotionally, spiritually, and even financially. I wanted to present Jesus and the leader who followed me with a healthy vision and organization. The best way to do that is to leave on a high note. God never works against Himself. He would never ask us to do something that damages or tears down the vision He gave us for our organizations. Our responsibility is always to leave people and things better off than when we left them, and to provide a return on God's investment.

SET MILESTONES, NOT TIMELINES

When I sensed God was revealing a new vision for my life and ministry, I decided I would set no timeline for my departure from Mountain Lake Church. Instead, I established a set of milestones I needed to accomplish for a successful transition, and then designated time goals for each of them. The rate at which I could accomplish each milestone would determine the timeline of my transition.

The first milestone was to work to make the organization as healthy as possible upon my exit. This included both building up and pruning the leadership teams God had surrounded me with at Mountain Lake. I did not want to leave my successor with any unresolved personnel issues on our staff, or even on our lay leadership teams. I began to make staff adjustments, some small, and some large. We moved a couple of high-level staff to new seats on the bus. With my coaching and support, they began to thrive in their new roles. We added new members with higher competencies to our church's finance team. We hired a consulting firm to come in and audit all our financial and hiring practices, to ensure these systems were healthy, and establish new practices. We decided to close one of our struggling multi-site campuses, with a possibility of a relaunch in the future. These are just a few examples of ways I tried to avoid leaving my successor with "dirty work" early on in his tenure.

Making decisions like this on the way out of an organization requires a lot of character. Why? Often, after we've received a glimpse of a new future and a new vision, our minds and hearts jump to future possibilities immediately. It requires discipline to stay focused on the present and hand over our current post in a healthy way. It also takes longer. This is not easy. On the other hand, I must admit that it was freeing to make decisions without fear of losing my job! In those final days as a senior leader I often thought to myself: *What can they do? Fire me?* Once I realized God was leading me away from our church, I was surprised to find that I felt freed up to make decisions I had procrastinated on because of fear. You can try on that feeling for size right now by answering a simple question: If you knew you were leaving your organization in one year, and had no fear of losing your job, what decisions would you make? Here's a thought: *Why not make those decisions now?* Leadership requires the courage and the character to do what needs to be done, regardless of the perceived cost or outcomes.

Milestone two was to hand select my replacement. Because I was the founding pastor of Mountain Lake, and our bylaws allowed it, I had the opportunity to personally select my successor. This step is not always possible, but if the leader has stewarded the vision well during his or her tenure, usually, regardless of what the bylaws say, an organization will allow the current leader to speak into the selection of a successor.

This is the most important hire we could ever make. That's why I decided to inform a few trusted key leaders of my planned departure from Mountain Lake. I shared my thoughts on the traits I believed my successor would need, and asked those people to speak to them, challenge them, or affirm them. I invited these key leaders into the process of selecting my successor. After all, as with any change, if I couldn't get a few key leaders to buy in to a new pastor, how would I get the entire church to do so?

Milestone three was to go public. After the search for my replacement had already privately been underway for a few weeks, I went public with the church to let them know I would soon be transitioning off the platform. I decided that somewhere around a ninety-day notice would be sufficient to find the new leader, allow him to join our team, and get off on the right track. More importantly, this time period would give my church ample time to process the loss of their founding leader as well as celebrate all that God had done through us over the last sixteen years. My own family needed time to sort through all of our emotions and grieve letting go of the amazing organization we had founded and led for the past sixteen years.

The first stage of grief for many people is anger. I knew there would be hurt, confusion, and anger over the fact that I was leaving. I wanted to allow some time for people to process some of those emotions with me, instead of in my absence. During this time, we hosted dinners in my home, individual parties for each of my three children and their friends, and several church-wide events that allowed the church family to walk through all of this with us. During those ninety days, we threw a lot of parties, and we went out with a bang!

THE EXIT

Our family moved out of the community. I wanted to give space for the new pastor to establish his leadership and flourish without being forced to operate in my shadow. I cautioned him about making major ministry decisions or staffing decisions for at least the first few months of his tenure. My strongest counsel to him was to take those first few months and *earn* the right to lead our existing staff, and to love the rest of the leaders in our church. I went overboard to remind him that the most important decisions he would make during his early days would be the ones to love people well. People always want to be loved before they are led.

I handed the vision over to my successor, and rode off into the sunset. The new senior leader and I are still friends. We talk almost every week. The vision is still alive. The church is taking new ground. The process wasn't perfect, but the transition has worked! While I am proud of many achievements over the last sixteen years, I am most proud of the way I left. Our legacy is often marked by how we leave.

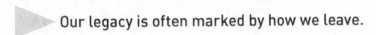 Our legacy is often marked by how we leave.

Leaving one vision to pursue another was the most difficult leadership decision I have ever made. I ran across a quote during my decision process that gave me courage to let go:

> *"Change is hard because people overestimate the value*
> *of what they have—and underestimate the value*
> *of what they may gain by giving that up."*[3]

I am so glad I made the decision to hand the vision off to someone else at just the right time. I stewarded the vision well up until my last day, I finished well because I was mean about the vision until the last day on the job. That's your job too!

Like it or not, you are serving right now in an interim position. How will you steward the vision beyond you? Will the vision outlive and outlast you? Are you planning now to leave? Are you planning your exit? You should. It's the best thing you could do for the vision. That's what I did, and I'm proud to say the vision has outlived me. My prayer for you is that God's vision would outlive you. Isn't that what you want?

In My Journal

▸ When was the last time I wanted to quit? Why?

▸ If I could do anything to my organization before leaving, without fear, what would it be?

▸ What is my plan for the vision to outlive and outlast me?

▸ What decisions am I making now that could work against that?

▸ What decisions do I need to begin to make now to prepare my organization to love beyond my leadership?

DON'T BE AFRAID

You may have seen the "Keep Calm and Carry On" images that have been so popular in the last few years on social media. Though most of us have seen the meme at some point, few of us know the story behind it. "Keep Calm and Carry On" was a motivational poster campaign led by the British government in 1939 in preparation for World War II. Around 2.5 million copies of this poster were printed in hopes of boosting morale among the British citizens as war loomed, but they never made it to posting. The movement was soon forgotten, out of sight and out of mind, until fifteen of the posters showed up on an episode of the *Antiques Roadshow* television series, and we know the rest. The movement went viral. Soon we began to see "Keep Calm and . . ." everything else. It eventually went silly crazy: "Keep Calm . . . and Eat Chocolate," "Keep Calm . . . and Go Shopping," "Keep Calm . . . and Use the Force." On and on it went.

The interesting thing to me is the timing of the resurgence of the Keep Calm campaign, because there has never been a time in history when people more need to keep calm than today. It seems as if the art of staying calm has largely been lost in our society. Instead, when presented with a challenging or anxious situation, most of us freak out! We go off. We vent on Facebook. We go ballistic, we commit road rage, we fight, we riot, we overreact, and we overstress. We worry about every little thing, *all the time*. The great need of our day is for some calm in the midst of the chaos.

There are already too many people making fear-based decisions. The world could use some leaders who are not ruled by fear. We simply cannot lead if we're making leadership decisions based on what will make everyone happy, or on who might leave or not leave, give or not give. The cry of our day is for courageous leaders, not cowardly leaders.

> The cry of our day is for courageous leaders, not cowardly leaders.

Do you know what the most common command in the Bible is? "Don't be afraid." God commands it to the Israelites, who are paralyzed with fear, caught between the Egyptians and the Red Sea:

Do not be afraid. Stand firm and you will see the deliverance the LORD will bring you today. (Ex. 14:13)

Don't be afraid. Stand firm. Trust that God is at work. See this through. Keep calm. That's good advice, isn't it? By the time we get to the book of Joshua, God adds to His command to not be afraid:

"Have I not commanded you? Be strong and courageous. Do not be afraid; do not be discouraged, for the LORD your God will be with you wherever you go." (Josh. 1:9)

God says: "Don't just keep calm. Be courageous. Don't just stand firm. Take new ground. Cross the Jordan. March around the walls of Jericho. Slay the giants. Fight My battles, My way, and you are ensured the victory every time."

I pray that as you have read the previous pages, God has been building one primary characteristic over all others: courage. I pray that you have felt new permission to make courageous decisions, have courageous conversations, make courageous calls, and be courageous about the vision God has given you. In the days ahead, I pray that you are more courageous, more passionate, and more intentional about the vision God has given you. So go out there and be mean about the vision!

Your friend and fellow leader,

Shawn Lovejoy

P. S. Our journey together doesn't have to end here. I love helping leaders work through whatever keeps them up at night. I love coaching leaders and pastoring pastors. If our time together in this book has encouraged you at all or helped you experience some breakthroughs, drop me a line at shawn@couragetolead.com. I'd love to hear your vision story!

NOTES

Chapter 1: Being Mean

1. Dictionary.com, s. v. "mean," accessed June 30, 2015, http://dictionary.reference.com/browse/mean?s=t.

2. Merriam-Webster Online, s. v. "mean," accessed June 30, 2015, http://www.merriam-webster.com/dictionary/mean.

Chapter 2: It All Starts with Vision

1. "Overview of Atlanta," North American Mission Board, accessed September 28, 2015, http://www.namb.net/atlanta/overview/.

2. Shawn Lovejoy, *The Measure of Our Success* (Grand Rapids: Baker Books, 2012).

Chapter 3: Vision and Success

1. Jim Collins and Jerry I. Porras, *Built to Last: Successful Habits of Visionary Companies* (New York: HarperCollins, 2011).

2. Ibid.

3. David Lumb, "Remember Apple's Lisa, the Computer that Cost Steve Jobs a Gig?" *Fast Company,* January 22, 2015, http://www

.fastcompany.com/3041272/the-recommender/remember-apples
-lisa-the-computer-that-cost-steve-jobs-a-gig-kevin-costner-d.
4. Collins, *Built to Last*, 16.
5. Ibid., 9.
6. Ibid., 8.
7. Ibid., 9.

Chapter 4: A Vision We're Willing to Die For

1. Will Mancini, *Church Unique: How Missional Leaders Cast Vision, Capture Culture, and Create Movement* (San Francisco: Jossey-Bass, 2008), 15.
2. Ibid., 84.
3. Ibid.
4. The John Maxwell Company, "7 Factors that Influence Influence," John Maxwell Leadership Blog, July 8, 2013, http://www.johnmaxwell .com/blog/7-factors-that-influence-influence.

Chapter 5: Keeping the Vision Alive in Me

1. Bill wrote about this in his book *Axiom: Powerful Leadership Proverbs* (Grand Rapids: Zondervan, 2008), Kindle edition, loc. 820.
2. Bill Hybels, *Leadership Axioms* (Grand Rapids: Zondervan, 2008), 58.
3. Henry Blackaby and Richard Blackaby, *Experiencing God* (Nashville: B&H Publishing Group, 2008), Kindle edition, loc. 3584-3585.

Chapter 6: Keeping the Vision Alive in Others

1. You can start with Luke 5:16, Mark 6:31, Matthew 14:23, Mark 6:45, Mark 1:35.
2. John Ortberg, *The Life You've Always Wanted: Spiritual Disciplines for Ordinary People* (Grand Rapids: Zondervan, 2009), Kindle edition, loc. 820.

Chapter 7: Identifying a Vision Hijacker

1. Dictionary.com, s. v. "hijack," accessed July 1, 2015, http://dictionary .reference.com/browse/hijack.

Chapter 8: Keeping the Vision from Being Hijacked

1. Jim Collins, *Good to Great: Why Some Companies Make the Leap . . . And Others Don't* (New York: HarperCollins, 2011), Kindle edition, loc. 991.
2. I mean this! Drop me a line at shawn@couragetolead.com and let me know how it goes.

Chapter 9: When It's Not Working Out

1. "Nick Saban on Mediocrity," *60 Minutes: Moment of the Week*, November 3, 2013, http://www.cbsnews.com/videos/nick-saban -on-mediocrity/.

Chapter 10: Getting Back On Track

1. John Maxwell, "Are You Really Leading, Or Are You Just Taking a Walk?" Leadership Wired Blog, August 7, 2012, http://www.john-maxwell.com/blog/are-you-really-leading-or-are-you-just-taking -a-walk.
2. To find out more, visit www.couragetolead.com.

Chapter 12: Releasing the Vision to a New Leader

1. William Vanderbloemen and Warren Bird, *Next: Pastoral Succession That Works* (Grand Rapids: Baker Publishing Group, 2014), Kindle edition, loc. 167–169.
2. Ibid., loc. 353–356.
3. James Belasco and Ralph Stayer, *Flight of the Buffalo*, quoted in Samuel Chand, *Leadership Pain: The Classroom for Growth* (Nashville: Thomas Nelson, 2015), 82–83.

ABOUT THE AUTHOR

Shawn Lovejoy is directional leader for CourageToLead.com. He loves coaching leaders and pastoring pastors and working with teams as they navigate their way through the vision. Shawn consults, coaches, and speaks to leaders all across the country about all things vision and team. He currently lives in Trussville, Alabama, (a suburb of Birmingham), with his wife Tricia, and his three kids, Hannah, Madison, and Paul.

CPSIA information can be obtained
at www.ICGtesting.com
Printed in the USA
LVOW07s1355050517
533168LV00010B/111/P